TRANSITION ISSUES

Helping young adolescents cope with some difficult personal and social problems they may encounter.

Written by

Maureen Hyland

Prim-Ed
Publishing
www.prim-ed.com

TRANSITION ISSUES (Ages 10+)

Published by R.I.C. Publications® 2005
Reprinted underlicence by
Prim-Ed Publishing 2005
Copyright© Maureen Hyland 2004
ISBN 1 920962 46 8
PR–0653

This book is dedicated to my Auntie Maureen who taught me that we never stop learning.

This master may only be reproduced by the original purchaser for use with their class(es). The publisher prohibits the loaning or onselling of this master for the purposes of reproduction.

Copyright Notice

Blackline masters or copy masters are published and sold with a limited copyright. This copyright allows publishers to provide teachers and schools with a wide range of learning activities without copyright being breached. This limited copyright allows the purchaser to make sufficient copies for use within their own education institution. The copyright is not transferable, nor can it be onsold. Following these instructions is not essential but will ensure that you, as the purchaser, have evidence of legal ownership to the copyright if inspection occurs.

For your added protection in the case of copyright inspection, please complete the form below. Retain this form, the complete original document and the invoice or receipt as proof of purchase.

Name of Purchaser:

_____

Date of Purchase:

_____

Supplier:

_____

School Order# (if applicable):

_____

Signature of Purchaser:

_____

Internet websites

In some cases, websites or specific URLs may be recommended. While these are checked and rechecked at the time of publication, the publisher has no control over any subsequent changes which may be made to webpages. It is strongly recommended that the class teacher checks all URLs before allowing children to access them.

View all pages online

http://www.prim-ed.com

FOREWORD

Every day, teachers are faced with children who are dealing with many issues, some beyond the control of the school situation, that can impact greatly upon the learning and general development of their children. Apart from being educators, teachers have to take on innumerable roles as they strive to encourage, support and protect the children within their care. They are there to help their children meet the challenges of both the school environment and the wider community.

This book is designed to help teachers, particularly in the upper primary and lower secondary levels, address a number of situations that, at some stage, may involve the lives of some or all of their children. The activities provide a framework for literacy-based, worthwhile discussion and sharing of thoughts and ideas.

Seven major issues are addressed:

- **bullying**
- **peer pressure**
- **death of a friend or relative**
- **drugs**
- **accepting people with 'differences'**
- **transition to secondary school**
- **marriage breakdown**

CONTENTS

Introduction	Teacher information .... v–vi
	Curriculum links .... vii–viii

Bullying	Teachers notes 1–2
	Where had my best friend gone? 3–4
	Worksheets 1–3 5–7
	A quiet target 8–9
	Worksheets 1–3 10–12

Peer pressure	Teachers notes 13–14
	The cost of trying to 'fit in' 15–16
	Worksheets 1–3 17–19
	Is it wrong to be chicken? 20–21
	Worksheets 1–3 22–24

Death of a family member or friend	Teachers notes 25–26
	How could I celebrate? 27–28
	Worksheets 1–3 29–31
	The empty desk 32–33
	Worksheets 1–3 34–36

Drugs	Teachers notes 37–38
	Injecting for survival 39–40
	Worksheets 1–3 41–43
	Just like my brother 44–45
	Worksheets 1–3 46–48

Accepting people with disabilities	Teachers notes 49–50
	Silent heroes 51–52
	Worksheets 1–3 53–55
	Just one of us 56–57
	Worksheets 1–3 58–60

Transition	Teachers notes 61–62
	Thoughts on transition 63–64
	Worksheets 1–3 65–67
	The weekly class meeting 68–69
	Worksheets 1–3 70–72

Marriage breakdown	Teachers notes 73–74
	Far away on Father's Day 75–76
	Worksheets 1–3 77–79
	It's all my fault 80–81
	Worksheets 1–3 82–84

Teacher information

In each of the seven listed areas (bullying, peer pressure, death of a friend or relative, drugs, accepting people with 'differences', transition to secondary school and marriage breakdown) there are two stories. All are fictitious yet very 'true-to-life'. The main aim behind the stories is to dispel a sense of 'I'm the only one going through this' for the children involved. Following each of the stories, there are three activity pages that can be used by both teacher and child to generate discussion or just as a means of personal outlet for the child.

In each case:

> **The first activity page** is directly related to the story. It asks the children about the characters and the situations involved.
>
> Often this form of direct removal from a situation, or a 'looking in from the outside', will encourage children to feel less threatened when sharing thoughts, ideas and experiences.
>
> **The second activity page** is more removed from the story and allows the children to make general statements about similar situations in their everyday lives or the lives of others.
>
> **The third activity page** is one that promotes freedom of expression and encourages the child to look for the positives in situations that are sometimes unpleasant, cause feelings of insecurity or are hard to deal with.

The stories and activities can be used at the teacher's discretion. Those related to bullying, peer pressure, transition, accepting people with differences and drugs could be used with groups or in whole-class situations. Those related to death and marriage breakdown may be used more effectively with individual children, depending upon the situation involved.

Although teachers will never have 'all the answers', this text will hopefully present them with avenues that will allow them, together with their children, to:

- dispel unacceptable behaviour,
- feel comforted and reassured during trying or uneasy times,
- believe help and support are always available when times seem tough or when feelings of isolation take hold.

Teacher information

Each issue dealt with in this book is supported by:

Teachers notes

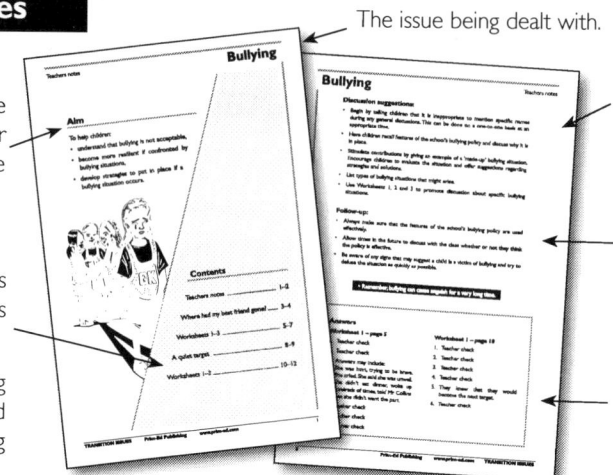

The aims of the issue are stated to guide the teacher as to how to help the children.

The titles of the two stories that share experiences relating to the issue.

Three worksheets relating to each story are detailed as well as corresponding teachers notes.

The issue being dealt with.

Suggestions on how to run discussion and points of interest are included.

Suggestions for easy follow-up points allow teachers opportunities to keep track of children who may be having difficulty in the issue area.

Worksheet 1 answers are provided. Answers for Worksheets 2 and 3 need to be decided by the teacher in discussion with the children.

Text

Two texts related to the issue are provided. Written to be emotive, they put the children in a position to be able to discuss their own thoughts and feelings.

Worksheets

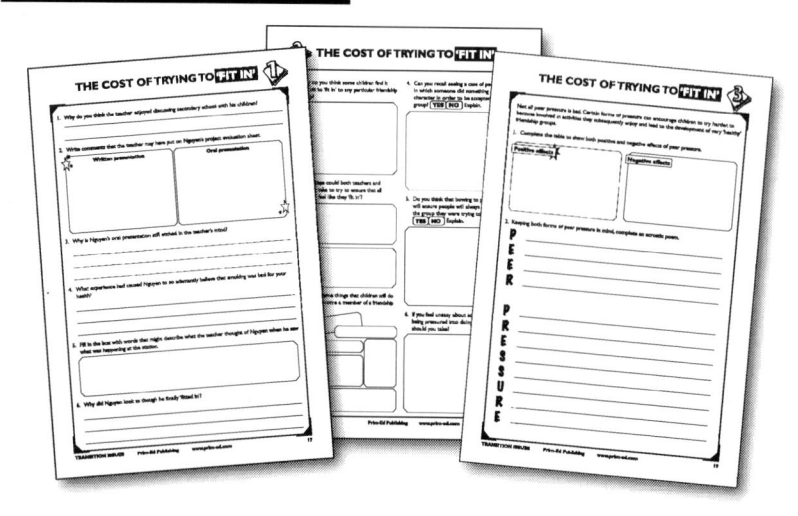

Worksheets have been provided to encourage children to think deeply about the issue, to consider possible outcomes and alternatives and to relate how they feel, or might feel, in the situation.

Answers are given for the first worksheet, as many answers may be obtained from the text. Worksheets 2 and 3 in each set provide opportunities for class discussion and individual responses.

vi   Prim-Ed Publishing   www.prim-ed.com   **TRANSITION ISSUES**

Curriculum links

Country	Subject	Level	Objectives
England	PSHE	KS2	• realise the consequences of anti-social and bullying behaviours on individuals and communities
			• know which commonly available substances and drugs are legal and illegal, their effects and risks
			• recognise the risks in different situations and decide how to behave responsibly
			• know that pressure to behave in an unacceptable or risky way can come from a variety of sources, including people they know, and how to ask for help and use basic techniques for resisting pressure to do wrong
			• realise the nature and consequences of teasing, bullying and aggressive behaviours and how to respond to them and ask for help
		KS3	• respect the differences between people
			• recognise the stages of emotions associated with loss and change caused by death, divorce, separation and how to deal positively with the strength of their feelings in different situations
			• recognise when pressure from others threatens their personal safety and well-being and to develop effective ways of resisting pressures
			• know about the effects of all type of stereotyping, prejudice, bullying and discrimination and how to challenge them assertively
Northern Ireland	PD	KS2	• know that pressure and influences can come from various sources such as peers and methods for resisting pressure
			• know about legal and illicit substances and drugs, their effects and the associated dangers
			• learn how to recognise, manage and express the feelings and emotions
			• recognise peer pressure can make them behave in certain ways
			• recognise bullying, its effects and how it might feel to be in someone else's shoes
			• recognise real friendship, how to respond to bullying and how to support peers in a positive way
Republic of Ireland	SPHE	5th/6th Class	• distinguish between legal and illegal substances, identifying those that are most commonly used and examine and understand the effects they can have
			• acquire the ability and confidence to identify, discuss and explore a range of feelings, especially those that are difficult to express
			• consider problems that can arise in friendships and how these could be handled
			• explore how the opinions, views or expectations of others can influence how people relate to each other, either positively or negatively
			• recognise, discuss and understand bullying and its effects
			• explore and discuss how individuals can deal with being bullied, knowing that others are being bullied and being a bully

Curriculum links

Country	Subject	Level	Objectives
Scotland	Health	D	• recognise the ways in which behaviour can influence people's relationships
			• show ways in which they can deal with change, e.g. transition from primary to secondary school
			• recognise that peer influences can affect choices they make
		E	• demonstrate responsible strategies to deal with a range of situations and emotions in relationships
			• recognise the impact of change on their lives, e.g. moving from primary to secondary school
Wales	PSE	KS2	• respect others and their uniqueness and recognise the importance of equality of opportunity
			• empathise with others' experiences and feelings
			• resist unwanted peer pressure and behaviour
			• develop strategies to resolve conflict and deal with bullying
			• begin to manage different emotions and handle change and new situations
			• recognise and understand the power of peer influence and pressure
			• understand the nature of bullying and the harm that can result
			• know about the harmful effects of legal and illegal substances
			• understand the changes in feelings at times of change and loss
		KS3	• empathise with others' experiences and feelings
			• be assertive and resist unwanted peer pressure
			• be aware of changing relationships in school situations and in the family
			• know the effects of and risks from the use of legal and illegal drugs

Teachers notes

Bullying

Aim

To help children:

- understand that bullying is not acceptable,
- become more resilient if confronted by bullying situations,
- develop strategies to put in place if a bullying situation occurs.

Contents

Teachers notes 1–2

Where had my best friend gone? 3–4

Worksheets 1–3 5–7

A quiet target 8–9

Worksheets 1–3 10–12

TRANSITION ISSUES   Prim-Ed Publishing   www.prim-ed.com

Bullying

Teachers notes

Discussion suggestions:

- Begin by telling children that it is inappropriate to mention specific names during any general discussions. This can be done on a one-to-one basis at an appropriate time.
- Have children recall features of the school's bullying policy and discuss why it is in place.
- Stimulate contributions by giving an example of a 'made-up' bullying situation. Encourage children to evaluate the situation and offer suggestions regarding strategies and solutions.
- List types of bullying situations that might arise.
- Use Worksheets 1, 2 and 3 to promote discussion about specific bullying situations.

Follow-up:

- Always make sure that the features of the school's bullying policy are used effectively.
- Allow times in the future to discuss with the class whether or not they think the policy is effective.
- Be aware of any signs that may suggest a child is a victim of bullying and try to defuse the situation as quickly as possible.

> • Remember, bullying can cause anguish for a very long time.

Answers

Worksheet 1 – page 5

1. Teacher check
2. Teacher check
3. Answers may include:
   She was hurt, trying to be brave. She cried. She said she was unwell. She didn't eat dinner, woke up hundreds of times, told Mr Collins that she didn't want the part.
4. Teacher check
5. Teacher check
6. Teacher check

Worksheet 1 – page 10

1. Teacher check
2. Teacher check
3. Teacher check
4. Teacher check
5. They knew that they would become the next target.
6. Teacher check

Bullying

WHERE HAD MY BEST FRIEND GONE?

Each week this year I had really looked forward to Wednesday afternoons. I was always happy going to school but I knew that I was in the group that the teachers called 'The Strugglers'. I found most of my work pretty difficult, especially spelling, reading and maths. However, I had such great friends that being in the same class as them just made every day at school worthwhile in some way.

Every Wednesday afternoon Mr Collins took us for drama. Sometimes we did simple plays. Other times we acted out songs or did miming activities. I absolutely loved it. I loved to sing and I loved to pretend that I was someone or something else. Mr Collins was the best teacher. He always encouraged us and made us feel that we were good at everything we did.

Three weeks ago he told us that he wanted to do a huge production for the whole school. We were going to do a presentation of *The sound of music*. Mr Collins spent most of the afternoon telling us the story of the Von Trapp family. He outlined the parts played by the various characters and even played a CD of some of the songs from the musical. At the end of the lesson, he told us that everyone in the class would be involved in some special way. Apart from the main characters, many of us would be in the chorus and others would be stage managers and ushers. He said that anyone who wanted to try out for a main character part would have to give him a letter by Friday afternoon. In the letter we would need to say which character we would like to try out for and why. I was so excited.

Before I went home that afternoon I tore a page out of the back of my English book and wrote Mr Collins a letter. In my letter I said that I wanted to try out for the part of Maria. Maria was the main character in *The sound of music* and she had many different songs to sing. My best friend, Monikka, was also going to audition for Maria and I think about four other girls as well.

Monikka and I had been in the same class since we started school and we did everything together. We often had sleepovers at each other's houses and she always helped me with my maths when I had problems.

During the lunch break and after school on the following Monday and Tuesday, Mr Collins held auditions. He said that we could sing anything we liked. I had learnt the song called 'My favourite things'. I loved the song and I thought that I sang it pretty well at my audition.

During our drama lesson on the Wednesday afternoon, Mr Collins read out the names of the children who would play the main characters. I thought it was just a dream when he said that I was going to be Maria. I was so happy I almost cried. I couldn't help but notice though, how disappointed Monikka looked. She didn't say 'Well done', like I expected she would. She just turned and looked away from me.

'This time I couldn't stop my tears. As I walked away I could see them laughing and joking about me.'

The next morning, during our French lesson, I could see a note getting passed around on a piece of yellow paper. I was a bit surprised when Tom passed it on to me and I saw my name written on the outside. Making sure that Madame Martinez was not looking in my direction, I unfolded the mystery letter. I felt sick in my stomach as I read it. 'You are such a stuck-up smarty Nadia. You think you are so good. Well, let's just see how pathetic MARIA is. You are sure to wreck our whole production.'

I might not be good at reading but I understood every word in the note and the worst thing was, I recognised the writing as Monikka's. I knew my face had gone very red and I could see half the class grinning in my direction. When I was brave enough to look across at Monikka I saw a look on her face that I had never seen before. My eyes were stinging as I tried not to

TRANSITION ISSUES   Prim-Ed Publishing   www.prim-ed.com   3

cry. I knew that would just make Madame Martinez ask me what the problem was. Fortunately, within about five minutes the bell went and everyone was allowed to go out for morning break. As I walked slowly towards the hooks to get my snack, I saw that my bag had been turned upside down on the corridor floor and everything had fallen out.

It was the worst break I had ever had. I just sat on one of the seats near the basketball courts, hurting from the inside to the outside. After a while, Anke and Samantha came and sat with me and asked me what was wrong. I just told them that I wasn't feeling well.

From break until lunchtime we worked on our history projects, and Monikka didn't come near me once. Until yesterday we had shared our resource books and helped each other with our headings and borders. I think Mrs Armstrong, our classroom teacher, realised that something was wrong because she kept looking over at me. At least I thought she did.

At lunchtime I thought that I'd be brave and I went down to where we always played netball. Monikka and Salvio were the captains and they began picking the teams. Everyone was chosen except for me. When I was the only one left, Monikka turned to me and said, 'Our teams are even. We can't have an odd number. You can't play, *Maria*.' That was so unfair. We had always played with odd numbers in the past. This time I couldn't stop the tears. As I walked away I could see them all laughing and joking about me. I went and sat by myself in a corner near the library. I think I cried for the next 30 minutes. As we walked into the classroom, Mrs Armstrong came up and asked me what was wrong. She could obviously tell that I had been crying. I could see Monikka absolutely glaring at me so I wasn't brave enough to tell the truth. Instead, I said that I was feeling really unwell. Mrs Armstrong sent a message to the office and it wasn't long before Mum was at the door to take me home. As soon as I saw her I burst into tears again. I told Mum that I had a very bad headache and a sore throat. Mum thought that Monikka was such a special friend that I couldn't tell her what was going on.

When I got home I went to bed. I didn't eat any dinner and I woke up a hundred times during the night thinking about the worst day of my life! I think I had just gone to sleep properly when I heard Mum telling me it was time to get up. What was I going to do? Could I still pretend to be sick? As I sat fiddling with my breakfast I decided that I was going to see Mr Collins and tell him that I didn't want to be Maria. I could tell that Mum was a bit worried about me but I told her that I was okay and that I just felt a little bit tired. When I got to school I went straight to Mr Collins' office. He was surprised to see me standing at his door and in his usual cheery way he said, 'And what brings you to my door so bright and early, Miss Maria?' Well, that was exactly what I didn't need to hear. I mumbled my way through a couple of sentences hoping that I was giving Mr Collins my intended message. He looked a bit puzzled but then concerned as a stream of tears rolled down my cheeks. I knew he was desperate to know exactly what was going on, but as a picture of Monikka's 'new face' flashed into my mind, I ran from the room.

— ✦✦✦ —

WHERE HAD MY BEST FRIEND GONE?

Worksheet 1

1. List words that highlight how Nadia was feeling prior to the auditions and after Mr Collins outlined who would be the main characters.

Prior to auditions	After characters were announced

2. Why do you think Monikka reacted the way she did?

   _____
   _____
   _____

3. What effect did Monikka's reaction have on Nadia?

   _____
   _____
   _____

4. Should Nadia have spoken truthfully to the following people as soon as the situation began getting nasty?

Monikka	Mr Collins	Her mum	Madame Martinez	Mrs Armstrong
YES NO	YES NO	YES NO	YES NO	YES NO

5. In your opinion, should the teachers have quizzed Nadia a little more about why she seemed upset and preoccupied?

   YES NO Explain.

   _____
   _____
   _____
   _____

6. After Nadia ran from Mr Collins' office, what do you think he would have done?

   _____
   _____
   _____
   _____
   _____
   _____
   _____

TRANSITION ISSUES   Prim-Ed Publishing   www.prim-ed.com

Worksheet 2: WHERE HAD MY BEST FRIEND GONE?

1. In this story, jealousy seems to have been the key to the bullying. Do you think that jealousy is a factor in most bullying situations? [YES] [NO] What other 'feelings' can lead to the development of bullying situations?

2. Is it easy to be dragged into a bullying situation without being a 'main player'; e.g. passing letters around, not letting people join in games? [YES] [NO] Explain.

3. Have you ever witnessed a bullying situation? [YES] [NO] If so, how did it make you feel?

4. Why do you think that children do not always report bullying to teachers or other adults?

5. If you were the victim of a bullying situation, what steps would you take to overcome the problem?

6. Do you think anyone can become a 'bully' or do you think such people generally have a particular personality?

WHERE HAD MY BEST FRIEND GONE?

1. Most schools have a special policy regarding bullying. Imagine that you are the headteacher of a new school and one of your first jobs is to draft such a policy. In the space below, outline your policy.

   General statement about ensuring that the school is a safe and happy environment for all.

   Reasons for instigating the policy.

   Contents of the policy.

2. Write a short comment about the Bullying Policy at your school and how you feel about its contents.

   _____
   _____
   _____
   _____

Bullying

They really had him cornered. By this stage Remi had started to cry, which only increased their determination to humiliate him.

A QUIET TARGET

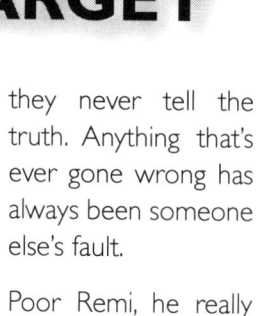

Remi was always pretty quiet. He never really got into trouble and he never really stood out for a particular reason. He just went about his school day doing his work and spending break and lunchtime with his two friends, Shamal and Troy. They were always on the tennis courts. It was the only sport they really enjoyed.

Last Friday, both Shamal and Troy were absent from school. This had never happened before and Remi, you could see, felt instantly alone. It wasn't so bad during class time because Mr Fijalski didn't give us a spare minute. We had three tests before break. However, when the bell went to go outside, Remi really dragged his feet and the familiar blue bat was nowhere to be seen. He sauntered down to the tennis area and sat on one of the benches.

Like iron filings are attracted to magnets, we watched as Tan, Adam, Dorina and Benjamin headed straight for Remi. This group had always believed they were superior to the rest of us and always had smart things to say. Since they were about six they have been the 'bosses' in our Year level. They've always been a group of four and no-one else has ever been allowed to join them. The worst thing is, they never tell the truth. Anything that's ever gone wrong has always been someone else's fault.

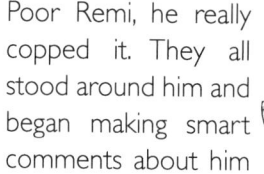

Poor Remi, he really copped it. They all stood around him and began making smart comments about him being a loner and asking him where his little boyfriends were. He tried to ignore them but Adam flicked his hand at his snack and sent chocolate cake flying in all directions. As they saw Mrs Wakhlu heading in their direction on playground duty, the four of them merrily went on their way, leaving poor Remi to scrounge up the chocolate mess.

As soon as Mrs Wakhlu turned towards the other end of the playground they were back and in full swing. They'd collected two bats and a tennis ball from the sport cupboard (which was out of bounds at break and lunchtime). Asking Remi if he wanted to play tennis, they began hitting the ball into him.

As soon as one had done it, another would grab the ball and do the same thing. They really had him cornered. By this stage Remi had started to cry, which only increased their determination to humiliate him.

Every time he tried to walk away, one of them would run in front of him. They were saying things like, 'Remi wants his Mummy' and 'Poor thing dropped his yummy cake'.

Suddenly, they looked in our direction. Beth and I felt really bad that we'd been standing watching what was going on. Remi wasn't really a close friend but he was a nice kid and we hated seeing this happen to him. But, we just knew that we couldn't interfere.

Once they'd seen us watching, the problem increased. If we had planned to tell a teacher beforehand, there was no way we could do it once they had seen we were witnesses. We knew that we would become their next targets.

As the bell went they left Remi and quickly made their way towards us. They warned us not to even think about mentioning the event to anyone or we'd be in trouble. What could we do? We'd been on the receiving end from these four in the past and it's not something you want to encourage. Remi came and joined the end of our line and he looked really distraught. He was probably contemplating what lunchtime might bring.

Tan, Dorina, Adam and Benjamin were all in another class but they watched us until we were right inside our classroom door. While we were doing a group mathematics project, Beth and I told Carly and Sean what had gone on at break. Sean's parents had already been up to see the headteacher because of the way he had been treated by Adam and Benjamin. He said that we had to tell Mrs Wakhlu or Mr Fijalski because this group was continually bullying someone.

Beth and I now faced a real dilemma. There would be consequences for poor Remi (and probably others) if they were allowed to keep up their tactics. There would probably be consequences for us to face if they found out we had reported them.

What should we do?

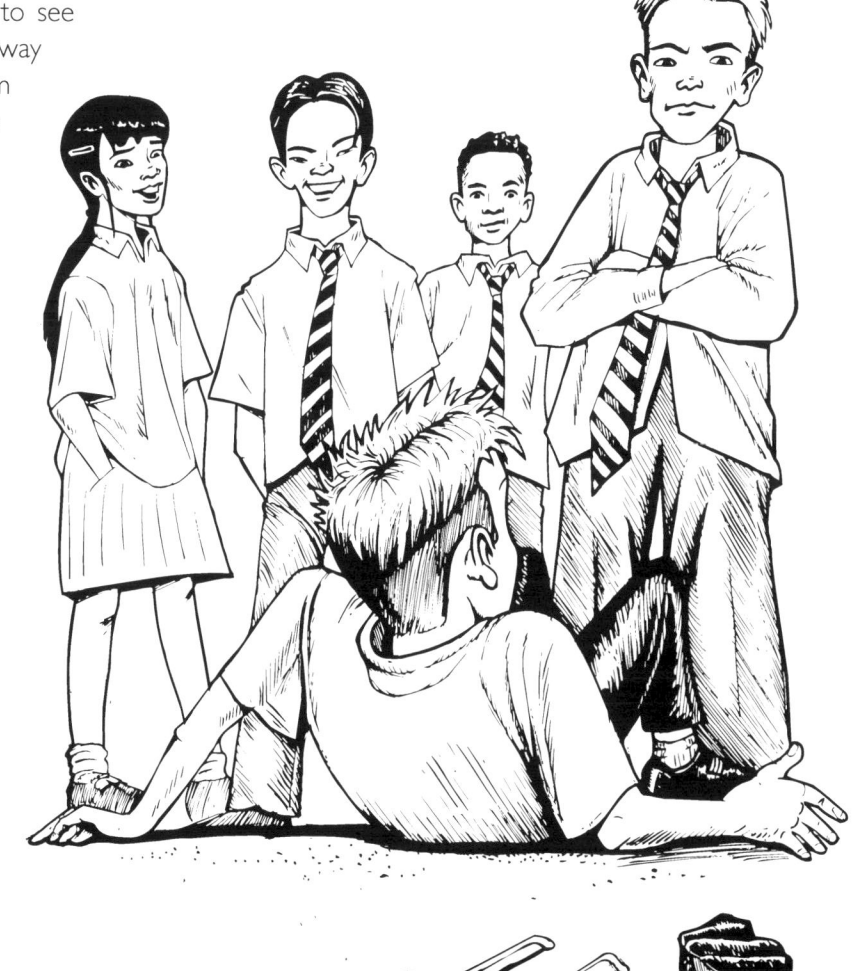

A QUIET TARGET

1. Remi was obviously lonely when Shamal and Troy were away. How does this highlight the value of being able to mix with more than just a small group of friends?

   _____
   _____
   _____
   _____
   _____

2. The following are reasons why people tend to bully others. According to what you think, number them 1–5, with 1 being the most common reason someone bullies another.

   - jealousy ☐
   - wanting to prove oneself to peers ☐
   - having been a victim of bullying ☐
   - angry reaction to a situation ☐
   - a desire to belittle another ☐

3. Were the people who stood and watched what was happening to Remi just as bad as the four who were inflicting the actual punishment?

   [YES][NO] Explain.

   _____
   _____
   _____

4. With what you know about bullying situations, how would you rate the reaction of those who stood and watched what was going on?

   |——————————————————|——————————————————|
   most unusual   **very typical**

5. Why were the girls feeling reluctant to report the bullying episode?

   _____
   _____
   _____
   _____

6. Why do you think Sean was so adamant that the girls should report what they had seen?

   _____
   _____
   _____
   _____
   _____

A QUIET TARGET

Worksheet 2

1. In the story, Remi was a victim of both verbal and physical bullying. Do you think one form of bullying is worse than the other form or can they be equally damaging? Explain.

   _____
   _____
   _____

2. Do you think quiet children are more likely to be a target for bullies than those with outgoing personalities? [YES] [NO] Explain.

3. In the playground, how do you think teachers could help alleviate problems such as the one outlined in the story?

   _____
   _____
   _____

4. Obviously, a fear of reprisal made the girls reluctant to report the bullying. Is this a good enough reason not to inform teachers of such occurrences? [YES] [NO] Explain.

   _____
   _____
   _____

5. If you were afraid to be seen telling a teacher or another adult about a bullying situation, how else could you get the message across?

   _____
   _____
   _____
   _____

6. Do you think people who bully others can change and become responsible for their behaviour? [YES] [NO]
   If yes, how might this come about?

   _____
   _____
   _____
   _____

TRANSITION ISSUES   Prim-Ed Publishing   www.prim-ed.com

A QUIET TARGET

Worksheet 3

1. If children are found to be bullying others at school it is important that the parents are notified about what has taken place. Taking on the role of a classroom teacher, write a letter to parents informing them of inappropriate behaviour in which their child has been involved. In the letter outline the issue, the hurt it caused and the subsequent punishment that is to take place.

2. Create an 'anti-bullying' slogan that you could enlarge and have displayed in a prominent position in your school.

Prim-Ed Publishing   www.prim-ed.com   **TRANSITION ISSUES**

Teachers notes

Peer pressure

Aim:

To help children:

- understand that peer pressure can have both positive and negative effects on an individual,
- understand that peer pressure can be executed in different ways,
- identify when they are being put in a compromising position,
- develop strategies that will help them make appropriate decisions when confronted by peer pressure situations.

Contents

Teachers notes 13–14

The cost of trying to 'fit in' 15–16

Worksheets 1–3 17–19

Is it wrong to be 'chicken'? 20–21

Worksheets 1–3 22–24

Peer pressure

Teachers notes

Discussion suggestions:

- Begin by telling children that it is inappropriate to mention specific names during any general discussions. This can be done on a one-to-one basis at an appropriate time.
- As a class, list some positive and negative effects of peer pressure.
- Ask children what they think are situations in which they could be confronted by peer pressure.
- Discuss why people might become prone to asserting unnecessary/unwanted pressure on others.
- Use Worksheets 1, 2 and 3 to promote discussion about specific peer pressure situations.

Follow-up:

- Take time in the future to 'revisit' points raised during class discussions.
- Have children debate the topic, 'Everyone at some stage will be confronted by peer pressure'.
- Be aware of any signs that may suggest a child is being a victim of peer pressure and, if not consulted, intervene before the situation escalates.

- **Remember, peer pressure can have both positive and negative effects on an individual.**

Answers

Worksheet 1 – page 17

1. Teacher check
2. Teacher check
3. He graphically described the effects of smoking and quoted amazing statistics without relying on his cue cards. He spoke with conviction.
4. His favourite uncle died of lung cancer.
5. Teacher check
6. People appeared to want him and he looked as if he felt important.

Worksheet 1 – page 22

1. Teacher check
2. They questioned if he was a 'chicken', implied he was an immature baby, and threatened his membership of their special friendship trio.
3. Teacher check
4. Teacher check
5. Teacher check
6. Teacher check
7. Teacher check

THE COST OF TRYING TO 'FIT IN'

I loved teaching the final year of primary school and I loved discussing with my children their feelings about stepping out into 'the world of secondary school', a world so much more diverse than that of our primary school environment. Sharing with them their views on various social issues was always enlightening and often made me wish that I could meet up with them all 10 years down the track to find out about the pathways their lives had taken.

I can remember one year we spent a term studying the human body. We looked at its various systems and investigated ways in which we could protect the development of our bodies. Even as the teacher I learnt many interesting facts that I hadn't known before, like how many bones we have and how long the small intestines are.

As part of this unit of work the children had to research and present a written project and deliver an oral presentation about actions or habits that could affect the overall development and health of the body. Some children looked at diet. Others studied exercise and fitness. Nguyen chose to research the effects of cigarette smoking on the human body.

Nguyen was a relatively quiet boy. He was a deep thinker who seemed to wander in and out of friendship groups, never really seeming to have a best friend and often giving the appearance that he battled to 'fit in'.

I can remember correcting his written project and being very impressed by the research he had obviously done. He wasn't into decorative headings or artistic presentations but I can recall giving him a very good mark for the information that he included. However, it was his oral presentation that still remains very much etched in my mind.

As he stood in front of the class I was aware of the fact that he had prepared the suggested cue cards but he hardly used them. He looked up the whole time, not really focusing on the audience but gazing out into a distant space. The first part of Nguyen's presentation addressed the composition of a cigarette. He then went on, quite graphically, to explain the effects that smoking could have on the various parts of the body such as the lungs, the heart and the skin. He followed this up by quoting some amazing statistics related to sickness and death as a consequence of smoking. I was quite stunned that he could do all this without relying on his cards. The final part of his delivery consisted of a very strong message directed towards everyone who was listening – 'Take up smoking and you're gambling with your life! Cigarettes are nothing but 'coffin nails'!' His presentation was outstanding and one that I wished I had videoed to show the following year.

At parent teacher interviews the following week I told his mum and dad how impressed

I was, not only with the information he presented but the conviction with which he delivered his message. They had gone on to explain to me that Nguyen's favourite uncle had died of lung cancer. He had been a smoker for many years.

One afternoon the following year I was dropping off my son at the local railway station. It was early in the second term and it was just at the time when many of the secondary school children arrived back at Northburn Station after a day at school. I sat for a moment studying the various uniforms and just looking, almost subconsciously, at the different sizes, styles and personalities portrayed by these young children.

Suddenly, I spotted Nguyen standing with a group of about 10 others. There were both boys and girls in the group and they were very busy discussing things related to school bags and uniforms. I was really quite horrified when I saw one of the girls hand Nguyen a cigarette. He had a couple of puffs and then passed it on to the boy standing on his left. I felt unable to leave as the scene made me feel quite betrayed and in a sense, let down. Within a short time the very small remains of the cigarette were tramped into the ground by one of the boys but it had obviously proved insufficient for their cravings. I was stunned to see Nguyen go ferreting around in his school bag and then present the group with a new pack of what a year ago he had called 'coffin nails'. For once Nguyen looked part of a group. People looked as though they wanted him. He looked as though he felt important.

As I drove away that afternoon my mind was bombarded with questions. Was peer pressure responsible for children developing such bad habits? Had Nguyen been so desperate to feel accepted and valued that he had stooped to something he had vowed and declared he would never do? How did he get the cigarettes? Who gave them to him? Did his parents know he smoked? But the question that stayed with me for hours was – Did he ever think about his favourite uncle?

THE COST OF TRYING TO 'FIT IN'

Worksheet 1

1. Why do you think the teacher enjoyed discussing secondary school with his children?
   _____
   _____

2. Write comments that the teacher may have put on Nguyen's project evaluation sheet.

Written presentation	Oral presentation

3. Why is Nguyen's oral presentation still etched in the teacher's mind?
   _____
   _____
   _____

4. What experience had caused Nguyen to so adamantly believe that smoking was bad for your health?
   _____
   _____
   _____

5. Fill in the box with words that might describe what the teacher thought of Nguyen when he saw what was happening at the station.

   _____

6. Why did Nguyen look as though he finally 'fitted in'?
   _____
   _____
   _____

TRANSITION ISSUES   Prim-Ed Publishing   www.prim-ed.com   17

THE COST OF TRYING TO 'FIT IN'

Worksheet 2

1. Why do you think some children find it difficult to 'fit in' to any particular friendship group?

2. What steps could both teachers and children take to try to ensure that all children feel like they 'fit in'?

   TEACHERS

   CHILDREN

3. What are some things that children will do to try to become a member of a friendship group?

4. Can you recall seeing a case of peer pressure in which someone did something quite out of character in order to be accepted as part of a group? **YES** **NO** Explain.

5. Do you think that bowing to peer pressure will ensure people will always be part of the group they were trying to impress? **YES** **NO** Explain.

6. If you feel uneasy about something you are being pressured into doing, what action should you take?

THE COST OF TRYING TO 'FIT IN'

Not all peer pressure is bad. Certain forms of pressure can encourage children to try harder, to become involved in activities they subsequently enjoy and lead to the development of very 'healthy' friendship groups.

1. Complete the table to show both positive and negative effects of peer pressure.

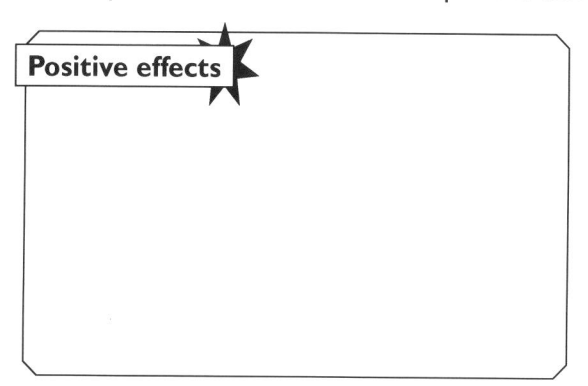

Positive effects	Negative effects

2. Keeping both forms of peer pressure in mind, complete an acrostic poem.

P _____
E _____
E _____
R _____

P _____
R _____
E _____
S _____
S _____
U _____
R _____
E _____

Within no time, the other parents of the 'missing' boys were at the school.

IS IT WRONG TO BE 'CHICKEN'?

TOBY HAD MANY FRIENDS at school, but Mario and Erik were by far the closest. They were all pretty well behaved at school, although occasionally they'd been in trouble for delaying their return to class once the bell had gone. They'd also done stupid things like taking down artwork and hanging it back upside down, or changing everyone's name tags on their desks when a student teacher had come to take a lesson.

Mario and Erik lived next door to each other and they walked to and from school together every day. It was usually the two of them who planned the devilish deeds, but Toby always willingly complied with their plans.

One day, the two of them came to school with an idea that instantly sent shudders down Toby's spine. Although he really enjoyed being part of their usual pranks, they were generally harmless deeds that most people would regard as funny. But he was not so sure about the latest plan.

Mario and Erik told him of their plan to wag school the next day. They were going to leave home at the usual time but instead of going to school, they were going to catch the train into the city. They would return in time to get home by their usual 4 o'clock. They told Toby that they would meet him at the station.

Toby felt sick. This was something well beyond fun and games. The other two boys were quick to sense his uneasiness. After questioning whether he was 'chicken' or not they began to imply that he was an immature baby. How could he prefer a day doing maths, English or science to a day exploring the city? They said that if he didn't turn up he would no longer be a part of the special friendship trio.

Fortunately, the bell went and they had to go into class. Toby couldn't concentrate on his work and every time he glanced up he could see the other two boys staring at him. Eventually, after non-stop pressure all day, he told them that he would meet them at the station.

At nine o'clock the next morning, the three boys were on a city-bound train. When Mr O'Connell, their teacher, marked the attendance register he thought it was a little strange that all three were absent but concluded that perhaps they'd caught some sort of 'bug' from each other. Nothing else was thought about their absence—until Erik's mum arrived at school at about 12 o'clock. Erik had left his lunch at home.

There was instant panic. The rest of the class quickly became aware of the concern expressed by both Mr O'Connell and Erik's mum. The other two boys were mentioned very early in the conversation. When the other children in the class were quizzed by their teacher, Jean very innocently mentioned that she'd seen Toby crossing the ramp near the station when she was on her way to school. She had to stop and think a little when Mr O'Connell asked whether he was with anyone else and whether he was wearing school uniform. She was fairly sure that he was in school uniform, but she couldn't remember seeing anyone else with him.

A few very quick phone calls were made from the office. The concern increased when it became obvious that all three boys had left home that morning to come to school. Within no time, the parents of the other 'missing' boys were at the school. Mr O'Connell and Ms Di Luca, the headteacher, spoke to them all for a lengthy period out in the corridor. The word 'police' was mentioned several times but in the end it was decided more than likely that the boys would try to get home around the time that school was due to finish.

Sure enough, when the three boys alighted from a train at 3.30 that afternoon, there were six parents standing there waiting for them. A day that had been filled with fun and new experiences was suddenly filled with reprimands and demands for explanations. Toby felt the same sickening sensation he'd had when Erik and Mario had first outlined their plans to him. He had bowed to peer pressure and was now about to face the consequences.

Worksheet 1: IS IT WRONG TO BE 'CHICKEN'?

1. Why do you think Toby felt uneasy when Mario and Erik told him of their plans to wag school?

   _____
   _____
   _____

2. How did the boys pressure Toby into making a decision?

   _____
   _____

3. Do you think in making the decision to wag school, Toby really agreed with the plan?
   [YES] [NO] Explain.

   _____
   _____
   _____

4. List two words you would use to describe each of the following:

   (a) Toby's general attitude to school
   (b) Toby's ability to make his own decisions
   (c) Erik and Mario's understanding of 'friendship'
   (d) Erik and Mario's ability to exert peer pressure

5. Should the teacher have carried out some form of investigation when he discovered the three very close friends were all absent on the same day? How might this have changed the situation?
   [YES] [NO] Explain.

   _____
   _____

6. What thoughts would have gone through Erik's mum's mind when she heard that Erik had not come to school?

   _____
   _____

7. How do you think the three boys felt when they stepped off the train and saw their parents?

   _____
   _____

Prim-Ed Publishing   www.prim-ed.com   TRANSITION ISSUES

IS IT WRONG TO BE 'CHICKEN'?

Worksheet 2

1. For what reasons do you think people put pressure on their peers to take part in unacceptable and irresponsible behaviour?

   _____
   _____
   _____
   _____
   _____
   _____

2. Why do you think some people give in to the wrong form of peer pressure and do things that perhaps they would never have thought of doing?

   _____
   _____
   _____
   _____
   _____
   _____
   _____

3. In what ways can peer pressure have favourable consequences?

   _____
   _____
   _____
   _____
   _____
   _____
   _____

4. Should the punishment be the same for children who plan a wrongful deed and those who tag along because of pressure applied to them?
   [YES] [NO] Explain.

5. If you are ever put in a situation where you are encouraged by others to do something you know is wrong, what could you do to avoid falling into their trap?

   _____
   _____
   _____
   _____
   _____
   _____

6. Do you think there is a certain type of person who is more susceptible than others to being pressured by his/her peers?
   [YES] [NO] Explain.

TRANSITION ISSUES   Prim-Ed Publishing   www.prim-ed.com

Worksheet 3: IS IT WRONG TO BE 'CHICKEN'?

1. Slogans hanging in a classroom can really alert children to positive behaviour. In the spaces below, create and decorate slogans or statements to highlight that people in your classroom will not tolerate unpleasant peer pressure.

2. In the first box, draw a picture of someone feeling intimidated by peer pressure tactics and in the second box, write about how the problem could be solved.

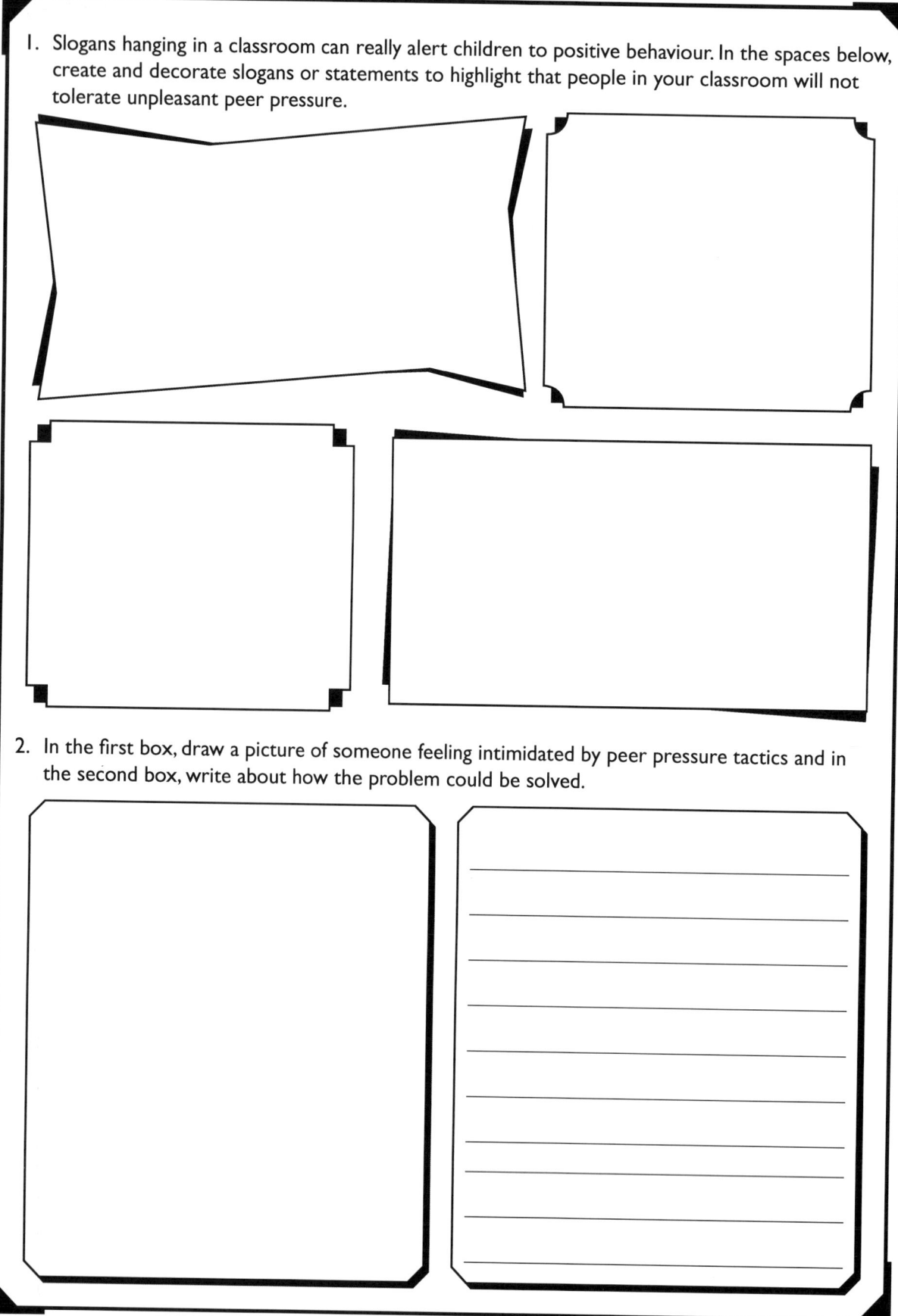

Teachers notes

Death of a family member or friend

Aim:

To help children understand that:
- death can occur when least expected,
- grieving takes a variety of forms,
- people grieve in different ways and for different periods,
- there is always someone to talk to when going through a grieving time.

Contents

Teachers notes 25–26

How could I celebrate? 27–28

Worksheets 1–3 29–31

The empty desk 32–33

Worksheets 1–3 34–36

Death of a family member or friend

Teachers notes

Discussion suggestions:

- Begin by telling children that it is inappropriate to mention specific names during any general discussions. This can be done on a one-to-one basis at an appropriate time.
- Ask children if they have been affected by the death of a friend or relative.
- Discuss different causes of death; e.g. old age, accident, disease.
- Have children list words that could express feelings at the time of a friend or relative's death.
- Ask the children who they think might understand the feelings of a grieving person.
- Use Worksheets 1, 2 and 3 where and when appropriate to promote discussion about specific situations relating to a death.

Follow-up:

- If children have been affected by the death of someone close to them, monitor their grieving process and offer support.
- Be prepared to seek further assistance if you remain concerned about a child's grieving process.
- If the situation involves the death of a fellow classmate, don't wipe the child from the memory of the class. At selective times, mention positive memories of the child.

- **Remember, children will grieve in different ways and for different periods.**

Answers

Worksheet 1 – page 29

1. He idolised his grandparents especially his Grandpa. The farm felt like another world.
2. Grandpa had changed from being vibrant and full of life. He looked tired and moved differently.
3. Teacher check
4. Jake felt like his heart had been torn in half when he was told that Grandpa had died.
5. No. He thought that Grandma needed Grandpa and so he must have been going to return to the farm. He stared at the coffin believing that Grandpa was only sleeping.
6. He felt destroyed, betrayed and angry. He hated Uncle Tom and everyone in the church for thinking it was a time to celebrate. He cried.
7. Teacher check.

Worksheet 1 – page 34

1–8.   Teacher check

How could I celebrate?

When it got to the last week of each term, Jake's mind was focused on one thing – going to spend a week with his grandparents. For as long as he could remember, he had spent the first week of every holiday at Grandma and Grandpa's farm at Bellington. His mum was able to have the second week off from work to be with him, but it was this first week that he looked forward to more than anything in the world.

The farm was only small. Most people would probably call it a 'hobby farm' but it was a place where Jake could go and really believe he was in another world. He idolised his grandparents, especially Grandpa, whom he had followed from paddock to paddock and from pen to pen during holidays for the past six years at least.

During Jake's last stay at the farm he knew he had taken on more responsibility than usual. On most occasions when he visited, he would spend time doing odd jobs with his grandfather and helping out wherever he could. However, during the last stay, Grandpa had asked him to do more things by himself. He fed most of the animals, moved the sheep from one paddock to the next and generally spent most of his time getting instructions from Grandpa and then carrying them out by himself.

For the first couple of days Jake had thought this was fantastic. He was now obviously old enough to take charge of some duties and this made him feel quite grown up. But it wasn't long before he stopped and looked at Grandpa and he noticed an amazing change in this man who was always so vibrant and full of life. Jake saw that he was looking tired and a strange weariness seemed to be reflected in all his movements.

Two weeks into the third term, Jake's mum had received a phone call from his grandma telling her that Grandpa had been taken to hospital. At last, they must be going to find out what was making him so tired, Jake thought. He was confident that when he went back to Bellington in eight weeks time, Grandpa would be back to his old self. Sadly, that wasn't the case. Grandpa was diagnosed with stomach cancer and he only lived for another five weeks. Jake did go to the hospital to visit him and he promised his grandfather that he would continue to visit the farm and help his grandma, but at the time the impact of his words didn't really register in his mind.

> Jake felt like his heart had been torn in half when he was told that Grandpa had died.

Jake felt like his heart had been torn in half when he was told that Grandpa had died. Visions of the two of them living the 'farm life' kept flashing before him. This was a man who had taught him so much, who had shared with him a passion for land and animals and who had been his inspiration for so many years. He couldn't be gone. And anyway, he thought, Grandma needed Grandpa. He must have been going to return to the farm.

Jake didn't say much to anyone for several days. He told his teacher what had happened, but life was very hectic as his mum and dad helped Grandma prepare for the funeral, so he seemed to live from day to day in a bit of a daze.

Sitting in the church on that Thursday afternoon, Jake could do nothing but stare at the coffin in which he believed Grandpa was only sleeping. He didn't really take in any of the first part of the service, but suddenly something happened that shocked him into reality just as though a bomb had exploded.

TRANSITION ISSUES

Jake's Uncle Tom walked to the pulpit and began to talk about why they were all in the church. 'This is a celebration ...' he began.

A celebration! A celebration! What was he on about, thought Jake. His grandpa was dead and someone was asking him to celebrate. This was unbelievable. He didn't hear the end of Uncle Tom's statement that actually said, '... of the life of a very unique person. A person who cared so much for others, who taught us innumerable things about life and who was, and who will continue to be, loved beyond all measure'.

The end of the statement was irrelevant to Jake. In a flash he realised that Grandpa was no longer sleeping. He was dead. He was never going back to the farm, and a church full of people was celebrating. He felt destroyed. He felt betrayed. He felt angry. The tears he couldn't control burnt his eyes and his throat was too tight to swallow. Even the warmth of Dad's arm around him could not bring back the security he had felt when Grandpa was alive. He hated Uncle Tom and he hated everyone else who sat in the church and didn't interrupt. How could so many people think this was a time to celebrate?

After the funeral, Jake felt that he was a different person living in a very different world. He became very quiet and only spoke to people when they specifically addressed him. He lost interest in his school work, he didn't visit his friends, he didn't want to go back to Bellington. He was hurting very badly inside and he couldn't understand why. Grief was something that had never been a part of his life and it was something he felt he couldn't control.

Jake's parents became very concerned about him. Eventually, his mum went and shared her concerns with the school psychologist. Mrs Morello arranged for Jake to have a meeting with a grief counsellor.

He was reluctant to go because he felt that too many people were interfering in his life. But after even the first meeting, Jake began to see things differently. He was able to look at what at happened from a different perspective. And he started showing signs of once again being the fun-loving person his grandpa had adored.

HOW COULD I CELEBRATE?

Worksheet 1

1. Why did Jake love going to the farm so much?
   _____
   _____

2. What did he notice about his grandpa during his final stay at the farm?
   _____
   _____

3. Rank the following:

   (a) Jake's usual feelings about visiting the farm.

   |⊢—————————————————⊤—————————————————⊣|
   indifferent   **very excited**

   (b) Jake's reaction to news of his grandfather's illness.

   |⊢—————————————————⊤—————————————————⊣|
   not accepting   **very accepting**

4. What sentence in the text explains how bad Jake felt when he heard that his grandpa had died?
   _____
   _____
   _____
   _____

5. Did he really accept the news that he wasn't going to see his grandfather any more?
   [YES] [NO]
   What information in the text tells you this?
   _____
   _____
   _____
   _____

6. How did Jake react when Uncle Tom began to speak at the funeral and why did he react this way?
   _____
   _____
   _____
   _____

7. Do you think it was important that Jake's parents made an appointment for him to see the grief councellor?
   [YES] [NO] Explain.
   _____
   _____
   _____
   _____

TRANSITION ISSUES Prim-Ed Publishing www.prim-ed.com 29

Worksheet 2: HOW COULD I CELEBRATE?

1. Why do you think we sometimes find it hard to really accept that someone has died?

   _____
   _____
   _____
   _____
   _____
   _____
   _____

2. Do you think it would be easier to accept the death of a relative or friend if they had been sick for a long time rather than if they died suddenly? **YES** **NO** Explain.

   _____
   _____
   _____
   _____
   _____
   _____

3. If you have had a close relative or friend die, make a list of words that describes the various feelings you had after hearing the news.

4. Sometimes, when a person loses a very close friend or relative, he/she goes through a period of feeling quite angry. Why do you think this might be?

   _____
   _____
   _____
   _____

5. It can often be detrimental to keep sad feelings hidden inside ourselves. What do you think would be the benefits of sharing your feelings with another person following the death of someone close to you?

   _____
   _____
   _____
   _____
   _____

Prim-Ed Publishing   www.prim-ed.com   **TRANSITION ISSUES**

HOW COULD I CELEBRATE?

Worksheet 3

1. Think about someone close to you who has died. If possible, find a photograph of that person. In the space below write about all the treasured memories you have of this person. You might like to attach the photograph or draw a picture of that special 'someone'.

2. If there were aspects of this person's character that you would like to have inherited or be able to emulate, what would they be?

3. If you had the opportunity to say one more thing to this person before he or she died, what would you have said?

A special counsellor came into our classroom to talk to us about what had happened.

THE EMPTY DESK

The sight of that desk when we walked into the classroom on Monday morning was devastating. When we left school on Friday afternoon we had 26 children in our class. Following the weekend we only had 25 children. Something had happened that none of us was prepared for. It was something that we believed just couldn't happen.

On Saturday morning Joe had gone to play cricket with our local Under 13 cricket team. Joe loved his cricket and was always practising his bowling well before the football season was over. We used to joke with him that one day he would be playing for his country. No wonder he was the school sports captain.

He played a great game on Saturday, taking four wickets for 23 runs. When the game was over he was eager to meet his mum because his family was going to his cousin's house where once again he'd be able to play cricket.

When his mum was unable to go to a cricket game she always picked Joe and his dad up directly across the road from the oval where he played. Apparently, when he reached the car on Saturday he remembered that he'd left his cap inside the clubrooms so, telling his parents he'd just be a minute, he turned and sprinted across the road—directly into the path of an oncoming car. The ambulance people were unable to save him.

We all just stared at his desk and the chair that was to remain empty. At our school we have a special grapevine system whereby the parents in any particular class are able to pass messages from one to another, ensuring that everyone is contacted about something if a special need arises. So by the time Sunday evening had arrived we had all been told of Joe's death. We were all shattered when we heard but nothing could have prepared us for the feeling that engulfed us as we walked into the classroom on Monday.

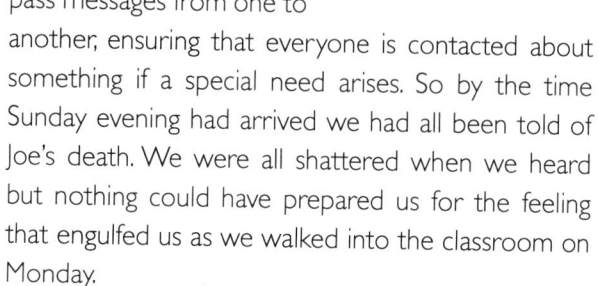

We have a full school assembly every Monday morning but on this day our teachers just took everyone straight into their rooms. The picture of tearful parents comforting each other and the sobs of children in the playground are sights and sounds we will never forget. It was just terrible in our classroom. Most children were crying. A few sat silently in their seats just staring into space and our teacher, Mrs Hadji, sat with her head in her hands. She was crying so badly. Everyone loved Joe so very much.

A special counsellor came into our classroom to talk to us about what had happened. Her name was Marie. Sadly, this was the type of occasion that she had been a part of on many occasions. Marie encouraged us to talk about the things that we could remember about Joe. Of course we talked about his love of sport and how, although he was in 'Gold House', he encouraged everyone at the school sports. We talked about the great fun he had when he pretended to be Elvis in a concert on school camp. Someone mentioned how hard he found it not to talk in class, especially when we were having a test. Others spoke about how he often carried his little sister's bag home from school.

Many of the things that people mentioned made us smile. Some people though, couldn't bring themselves to say anything.

Later in the day we had a special assembly in the school hall. Every class came. Our headteacher, Mr Stoner, told everyone about what had happened and he said some really good things about Joe. He read a poem to everyone that Joe had written in Term 1. It was called 'Give it your best shot' and of course it was about sport! At the end of the assembly one of the teachers put on a CD and we all listened to the song 'Reach for the stars'. Joe was always reaching for the stars. He tried his best at everything he did, even talking at the wrong time!

Our classroom had never been so quiet. It seemed like the energy had been zapped out of everyone. We didn't have to do any work. Mrs Hadji put a whole lot of activities out the front for anyone who wanted to do them. A few children did but most of us just sat talking in small groups.

Just before the bell rang to go home Marcus started crying really badly. Marcus is pretty tough and none of us had ever seen him crying before. Mrs Hadji went and sat right next to him and he told her how he was feeling very guilty because he'd had an argument with Joe on Friday. It was over something really simple like where they were hanging their school bags. We were pretty amazed when we heard Mrs Hadji tell Marcus that she was also feeling guilty. On Friday she'd kept us in for 10 minutes at lunchtime because Joe and a few others were talking at the wrong time.

Out of the blue, Sally spoke up. She hadn't said a word all day. She really doesn't talk much at any time but what she said was really special. She told us all that she thought we should think more about all the good days Joe had spent at school and about how much happiness he had brought to our class group. She said that these are the things she thought Joe would want us to think about. That was a pretty great thing for her to say and it really helped Marcus and Mrs Hadji.

Joe's funeral was yesterday. Our whole class went and so did many other children from the school. We all wore our school uniforms but we sat with our parents. The church service was very sad but at times it was also full of joy. A number of people spoke about our friend and every one of them had so many wonderful things to say. The hardest part was when Joe's dad spoke. He was really choking as he tried to talk. At the same time there was a video going behind him. It showed so much of Joe's life from when he was a baby right up until the last wicket he took at cricket on Saturday.

When the service was over our year group classes walked out of the church and formed a 'Guard of Honour'. As the funeral car drove slowly past us we each released two balloons, one gold and one blue. (They are our school colours.) All the children and their parents then went into the school hall for afternoon tea. It was the saddest of all days.

It's hard to think that things in our class will ever be back to normal. It's hard to think there'll ever be a time when we won't be thinking about what happened to Joe. It's hard to think that we will complete our school year in five weeks time without our very special friend.

TRANSITION ISSUES   Prim-Ed Publishing   www.prim-ed.com

Worksheet 1: THE EMPTY DESK

1. How do you think the children would have felt when they were first told about Joe's death?
   _____
   _____

2. Colour the words that you think describe Joe.

   | friendly | self-centred | enthusiastic | encouraging |
   | negative | self-motivated | caring | overpowering |

3. Why do you think the counsellor asked the children to talk about their memories of Joe?
   _____
   _____

4. List some activities that the children may have felt like undertaking that day.
   _____ _____
   _____ _____
   _____ _____

5. Should Marcus have been feeling guilty? [YES | NO] Explain.
   _____
   _____

6. What do you think of the comment that Sally made?
   _____
   _____

7. Why do you think the children released the balloons into the air?
   _____
   _____

8. What effect might Joe's death have had on the rest of their school year?
   _____
   _____

THE EMPTY DESK

Worksheet 2

1. Make a list of words that you think would describe your feelings if a close friend or classmate were to die.

2. What great fun times have you shared with your classmates that will remain etched in your memory forever?

3. Do you think it would be harder for you to accept the death of a young person than someone elderly? [YES | NO] Explain.

4. What questions do you think would come into the minds of children if one of their friends and classmates were to die?

5. When a tragedy, such as the one in the story occurs, how important do you think it would be for the fellow children to express their feelings to someone else? Why?

TRANSITION ISSUES Prim-Ed Publishing www.prim-ed.com 35

Worksheet 3: THE EMPTY DESK

1. Special memories should be treasured. Memories can sometimes help us cope with unforeseen circumstances that come into our lives. Recall and record a special memory from each age of your life.

Age 3	**Age 4**

Age 5	**Age 6**

Age 7	**Age 8**

Age 9	**Age 10**

Teachers notes

Drugs

Aim:

To help children:

- develop an understanding that some people need medication in order to improve their health and in some cases help them to survive,

- become aware of the fact that some drugs are illegal, addictive and very bad for their health,

- understand that there are avenues to follow if ever any drug situation concerns them.

Contents

Teachers notes 37–38

Injecting for survival 39–40

Worksheets 1–3 41–43

Just like my brother 44–45

Worksheets 1–3 46–48

TRANSITION ISSUES   Prim-Ed Publishing   www.prim-ed.com

Drugs

Teachers notes

Discussion suggestions:

- Begin by telling children that it is inappropriate to mention specific names during any general discussions. This can be done on a one-to-one basis at an appropriate time.
- Ask children why people sometimes have to take medication.
- As a class, make a list of different medications that the children know of and ask if they know for what purpose they are used.
- Talk about illegal drugs and ask children if they know of any in particular and if so, what effects they can have on a person.
- Use Worksheets 1, 2 and 3 to promote discussion about the use of medication and illegal drugs.

Follow-up:

- Ensure that asthmatics, and children requiring other necessary medication, feel comfortable taking their medication at school.
- If possible, have a doctor or a nurse speak to the children about the different effects of certain medications and illegal drugs.

• Remember to be fully aware of any medical needs of your children.

Answers

Worksheet 1 – page 41

1. She admired Joelina's appearance, clothes and taste in music.
2. Teacher check
3. Unacceptable outbursts of behaviour, a syringe in her bedroom; all her savings had been spent.
4. Teacher check
5. Adam is a diabetic.
6. (a) false (b) true (c) false (d) true (e) true
7. Teacher check
8. Adam will test his blood and inject himself with insulin twice every day. He will have regular checkups and be monitored by doctors.

Worksheet 1 – page 46

1. Teacher check
2. Teacher check
3. Underage drinking, taking an illegal substance (Ecstacy)
4. (a) There was no point in talking to him because he was spaced out.
   (b) Teacher check
5. Teacher check
6. Liam's behaviour may continue and the possiblity of growing up to be like him.
7. Teacher check

INJECTING FOR SURVIVAL

Just as Adam was about to inject himself with this giant needle, I woke up with Mum shaking me and calling my name.

MY COUSIN JOELINA was 15 and was referred to by most members of my family as 'that troublesome girl'. Up until about 12 months ago, Joelina had been my hero. I had wanted to look like her, dress like her and listen to the same music.

Quite suddenly, she stopped coming to our family functions and more and more frequently she became the subject of Mum and Aunt Sofia's conversations. I know they tried not to talk in front of me and often they seemed to speak in a strange code but I was clever enough to get the general idea of what was going on.

We'd had several lessons last year and again this year about peer pressure, friendship groups, drugs and alcohol etc. I remember Aunt Sofia telling Mum that Joelina was 'getting in with the wrong crowd' and how she'd been up to the school many times following some pretty unacceptable outbursts of behaviour by Joelina. I could always tell by the look on Mum's face and by her tone of voice that she was extremely concerned about her niece. Joelina was Mum and Dad's godchild and she had spent many holidays at our house. For years she had seemed like the sister I didn't have.

One night, I heard Mum telling Dad that after Aunt Sofia had found a syringe in Joelina's bedroom there was a really big fight. Apparently, Joelina was injecting herself every day with some drug. All the money that she had saved from her part-time job at the bakery had gone. I knew that she had been a very good saver because her major ambition had been to buy a car as soon as she turned 18. She had been saving money in the bank for the last three years.

For ages, there seemed to be endless family discussions about the damage Joelina had done to herself, where she was going in her life and the effect that she was having on everyone who cared about her.

I think it was because of all the talk about the drugs destroying her life and the fact that she was injecting herself daily, that I was truly freaked when Adam became sick. Adam, my younger brother, spent two weeks in hospital recently. He had developed this incredible thirst. One weekend he drank more water over two days than I would drink in a year. Mum and Dad, despite having no history of diabetes in either of their families, became very suspicious that this great thirst was a symptom of that disease.

Adam would have to inject himself twice a day, probably for the rest of his life.

After an early Monday morning visit to our family doctor, Adam was sent straight to Viewridge Hospital. He was subsequently diagnosed with diabetes and spent a number of days being 'stabilised' by the doctors. During this time he was taught how to test his blood and how to inject himself with insulin. Mum and Dad tried to explain all this to Jimmy, my other brother, and me.

The night that they told us all this information I felt a bit uneasy. Adam would have to inject himself twice a day, probably for the rest of his life. This thought must have been playing on my mind as I drifted off to sleep. I had the worst dream ever. I guess you'd call it a nightmare.

I dreamt that Adam was out in this dark lane with a big group of really rough people. They were all in weird moods. They were wearing T-shirts that said,

TRANSITION ISSUES   Prim-Ed Publishing   www.prim-ed.com

'Destruction is a Game' and they were passing around a syringe that seemed as big as a cricket stump. Just as Adam was about to inject himself with this giant needle, I woke up with Mum shaking me and calling my name. I felt sweaty and exhausted and absolutely terrified for my brother. What was going to happen to him? Were these two daily injections going to destroy his life?

I managed to mumble out some sort of story to Mum. Mainly because nothing was making sense to me, I don't think I made a huge deal of sense to her either. However, one thing that I said really had an impact on her. I said that I didn't want Adam to end up like Joelina. By the way that she gripped my shoulders, I knew that she had something pretty powerful to say to me.

'Adam's injections are nothing like your cousin's', she said. As I listened to her explain the effects of Adam's medication—and what would happen to him if he didn't have them—I became a little more relaxed. I think it was probably just that very word 'injecting' that had sent my mind into overdrive. Because we hear so much about people injecting themselves with dangerous drugs like heroin, I found it hard contemplating the fact that Adam could be injecting himself with anything that was going to do him good.

Mum explained to me that Adam would always be monitored by doctors, that his regular check-ups would guarantee that his prescribed medication was being effective and that he would be able to continue leading a normal life.

Horrible though the nightmare was, I guess I learnt a huge lesson about life. People are often given prescribed medication that is important for their survival. Other people misuse and damage their bodies by injecting themselves with harmful drugs. Thanks to Mum and my very disturbed sleep that night, I now understand that Adam and Joelina's situations are totally different.

— ✦✦✦ —

INJECTING FOR SURVIVAL

Worksheet 1

1. Why do you think the author had wanted to be like her cousin Joelina?
   _____
   _____

2. How and why do you think her attitude might have changed?
   _____
   _____

3. What were some of the indications that Joelina was doing things she shouldn't be doing?
   _____
   _____

4. Colour the words that could describe Joelina's changed personality.

cheery	withdrawn	moody	friendly
secretive	outgoing	mischievous	family-oriented

5. What was wrong with Adam?
   _____

6. Mark the following true or false.

   (a) Adam and Joelina had similar problems. **TRUE / FALSE**

   (b) Changes in Joelina's personality alerted her mother to her problem. **TRUE / FALSE**

   (c) Adam's personality was also likely to change. **TRUE / FALSE**

   (d) Injections are used for a variety of reasons. **TRUE / FALSE**

   (e) Some people rely on lifetime medication for quality of life and survival. **TRUE / FALSE**

7. Why do you think the author might have had the 'nightmare'?
   _____
   _____
   _____
   _____

8. How would Adam's condition be kept under control?
   _____
   _____
   _____
   _____

TRANSITION ISSUES   Prim-Ed Publishing   www.prim-ed.com

INJECTING FOR SURVIVAL

1. What do you think might be some warning signs to parents that their children are taking harmful drugs?

   _____

   _____

2. What is the difference between taking drugs prescribed by a doctor and unknown or non-prescribed drugs offered to you by another person?

   _____

   _____

3. List five conditions for which people may need to take prescribed drugs.

   a _____ **b** _____ **c** _____

   d _____ **e** _____

4. Labels on prescribed medications list important information. What information is printed on such labels?

   _____

   _____

   _____

5. Is it okay for someone to take medication that has been prescribed by a doctor for someone else? [YES] [NO] Explain.

   _____

   _____

   _____

6. What medications do you know of that people take for such things as headaches, colds and flu?

   _____

   _____

INJECTING FOR SURVIVAL

Worksheet 3

1. In the space below draw a picture of a medicine bottle. On the label write some important information that the user would need to read.

2. If a person is told by a doctor to take a particular type of medicine for life, what questions do you think he/she should ask the doctor?

3. Read the acrostic poem and then complete one of your own.

D Don't take drugs without a personal prescription from your doctor.
R Read information on the label.
U Use only as directed.
G Get help if problems arise.
S Seek medical advice before taking medication.

D
R
U
G
S

TRANSITION ISSUES Prim-Ed Publishing www.prim-ed.com 43

JUST LIKE MY BROTHER

There are four children in our family. I'm the third oldest. Liam is the oldest. He's 16. Sarah is 14, I'm 12 and Marty is nine years old. We've always been what most people would probably call 'average kids'. We've never given our parents too many grey hairs (well, not that many!), we've all been really healthy and, generally, we've been one big happy family.

Things have altered quite a bit over the last two months, however. Liam seems to have changed and terms like 'trying' and 'turbulent' have been getting mentioned more and more frequently in our house. Recently, Mum and Dad discovered that Liam had been going to other places instead of where he'd told them he would be. To get into some of these places you are supposed to be 18 years of age or over. He really got into trouble when they first discovered this, but last week there was a real 'explosion'. I was awake when Liam got home. He was dropped off out the front by someone and it was very late—something like two o'clock in the morning. Apparently, Mum and Dad were still sitting up waiting for him. He had told them that he was going to Stephen's to study, but when they rang there at midnight to say they were going to pick him up, they were told by Stephen's mum that he'd never been there. Stephen was sound asleep in bed after getting home from his job at the local supermarket.

As if Liam wasn't 'in for it' already—well, it got worse. When Dad opened the door, Liam was absolutely spaced out.

I know because I got out of bed and went into the lounge room when I heard Dad and Mum were really angry. I saw what he looked like. Eventually, Dad said that there was no point in talking to him while he was in that state and so he took him into his room and helped him get into bed. Mum was so upset.

Liam didn't go to school the next day because he was so unwell. Apparently, the whole story came out that day, though. Not

---

44   Prim-Ed Publishing   www.prim-ed.com   TRANSITION ISSUES

only had he been drinking alcohol but he'd taken two tablets called 'ecstasy'. I'd heard about these tablets on the news and someone had mentioned them during one of our drug education lessons at school. It made me get a very strange feeling in my stomach when I heard that my own brother had taken them.

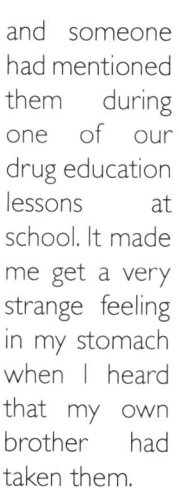

Liam had gone to this club with two other boys from his football team. They had been there on several other occasions. The other boys had already turned 18. Somehow, Liam had been able to get into the club even though he was underage. He admitted to Mum and Dad that he had drunk alcohol in the past, but he said that this was the first time he'd taken any tablets. His two friends had taken ecstasy tablets before and they told him that they gave you a really good feeling. Liam thought that maybe if he took some he'd feel really good for the science exam he had the following morning, but that really backfired. He couldn't even go to school let alone sit for the exam.

Twice since that night, Liam has been to see some counsellor with Mum and Dad. But what scares me is that he hasn't promised that he won't do it again. I'm finding that really hard to deal with. I'm also scared that I might fall into the same trap. For years, people have said things to me like, 'Aaron, you are just a replica of Liam' and 'It's great to see that you and Liam are such good mates. I'm sure you'll grow up just like him'. In the past, I'd loved it when people had said that. Now I almost resented it. We used to be great mates.

What if I do grow up to be just like he is?

TRANSITION ISSUES Prim-Ed Publishing www.prim-ed.com

JUST LIKE MY BROTHER

1. What do you think Aaron meant when he said they were just 'average kids'?
   _____
   _____

2. Why do you think the words 'trying' and 'turbulent' were being heard in the household?
   _____
   _____

3. What illegal things did Liam do?
   _____
   _____

4. (a) Why did the boys' dad just put Liam in bed that night?

   (b) Do you think that was the best thing for him to do? **YES** **NO** Explain.

   _____
   _____
   _____

5. What could have been the consequences of Liam's actions?

a	Staying out late
b	Going to 'over 18' places
c	Taking ecstasy tablets
d	Missing exams

6. What was it that Aaron was finding so hard to come to terms with?

7. Do you think there were any aspects of Liam's personality that Aaron would be happy to emulate? **YES** **NO** Explain.

   _____
   _____
   _____

46   Prim-Ed Publishing   www.prim-ed.com   **TRANSITION ISSUES**

JUST LIKE MY BROTHER

Worksheet 2

1. In the story Liam was obviously influenced by others. What types of people might try to encourage us to take drugs that are no good for us?

   _____
   _____
   _____
   _____
   _____
   _____

2. If someone did try to encourage you to take some form of drugs, write four answers that you could give them to show that you were not going to do as they asked.

   a.
   b.
   c.
   d.

3. Liam was given the drugs at a club. Where else might people try to encourage others to take drugs?

   _____
   _____
   _____
   _____
   _____

4. What effects can drugs have on your body and on your life in general?

   _____
   _____
   _____
   _____
   _____
   _____
   _____

5. If someone is asked to take 'drugs' who should they tell?

   _____
   _____
   _____
   _____

6. Do you think there is a certain age group that is really targeted by people trying to sell drugs? [YES] [NO]
   If so, what age group and why?

   _____
   _____
   _____
   _____
   _____

TRANSITION ISSUES   Prim-Ed Publishing   www.prim-ed.com

Worksheet 3: JUST LIKE MY BROTHER

1. Underneath each sentence write strategies you could use if confronted by the outlined situation.

a You are asked to go somewhere that is illegal for someone of your age.

b You are offered a cigarette, alcohol or illegal drug.

c A friend wants to tell her parents she stayed at your place when she didn't.

d You know that a close friend or relative is taking illegal drugs.

e You are feeling bored or lonely and are looking for a new challenge in your life.

f You are compared to a family member who does not impress you.

Teachers notes

Accepting people with disabilities

Aim:

To encourage children to:

- be accepting of people with disabilities,
- recognise that people with disabilities should not be isolated,
- develop an understanding of the different needs of people with different disabilities.

Contents

Teachers notes 49–50

Silent heroes 51–52

Worksheets 1–3 53–55

Just one of us 56–57

Worksheets 1–3 58–60

Accepting people with disabilities

Teachers notes

Discussion suggestions:
- Ask children if they know anyone with a disability.
- Discuss different disabilities and their effects.
- Talk about the wonderful things that people with disabilities can do.
- Outline some imaginary situations whereby a disabled child is to join the class. Ask the children what changes would need to be made.
- Use Worksheets 1, 2 and 3 to promote discussions about disabled people and the part they can play in our lives and society in general.

Follow-up:
- Read the story of Helen Keller to the class.
- Have children write to disabled athletes about their chosen sports.

- Remember, terms such as 'different' and 'dumb' are often very incorrectly used.

Answers

Worksheet 1 – page 53
1. They had not been seen on the pier before and they were different (strange).
2. Teacher check
3. Teacher check
4. They communicated by signing. They were not intimidated by the trio's imitation. They didn't react to the boys' screams.
5. Teacher check
6. They didn't hear the screaming because they were deaf.
7. They befriended the boys and realised how much they owed them.

Worksheet 1 – page 58
1. Andre had cerebral palsy which affected his muscular coordination and his speech. He needed a wheelchair.
2. Teacher check
3. Teacher check
4. Teacher check
5. Teacher check
6. They ensured that there was sufficient room for his wheelchair and that nothing obstructed it. They welcomed and included him by adapting games and assisting him.

SILENT HEROES

The scene down at the old pier this morning was the same as every other day of the holidays, except for one thing …

Josh, Tran and Sarita were at the very end of the 80-year-old pier, perched on their tatty canvas chairs. Their families had been coming to Huntington Bay for at least 10 years. The Hatman (so called because of the huge weatherbeaten hat that was always pulled down tight on his head and because no one actually knew his name) was sitting on his old cushion right next to a faded 'No Diving' sign. Roberto and Guiseppi had their gear on the rocks close to one edge of the pier—and then there were the 'newcomers'.

Almost at the end of the rickety old wooden sleeper construction, just to the left of The Hatman, sat two boys about 12 years of age.

Yes, they were strangers. Not only had they never been seen on the pier before, they had never been seen in Huntington Bay. And there was something unusual about the pair. They spoke not a word but communicated with each other by signing. They were obviously very used to fishing because they'd baited their lines and had them cast within five minutes of arriving. Their hands moved at an amazing pace as they 'talked' nonstop, laughing every now and then at something they both obviously found amusing.

Josh, Tran and Sarita had always regarded themselves as the dominant group on the little pier. They believed the school holidays were for them and that they had rights that nobody else had. Nobody ever dared to take their spot at the end of the pier and they rarely spoke to anyone else. They had been known to pass rude remarks about old Hatman and had even been seen kicking one of his buckets into the water. They often imitated Roberto and Guiseppi as they spoke to each other in their native language and this morning they felt quite delighted when they found they had new targets.

It wasn't a particularly profitable morning as far as fishing was concerned. In fact, the only person to reel in a catch was one of the newcomers. Quite a good-sized flathead pulling on the end of one of their lines had sent the hands of the other into incredible action. Obviously giving instructions or offering advice, the excitement was apparent on his face. Not so happy were the expressions on the faces of Josh, Tran and Sarita. There was an obvious feeling of jealousy building up. Perhaps it was due to the fact that their territory had been invaded. Perhaps it was because these newcomers had caught a fish that they believed should have been theirs. No matter what the reason, the three began waving their hands around at each other and looking mockingly at the two young boys, who proudly dropped their wriggling fish into a bucket of water. Within no time the actions of the trio had become very obvious to the rest of the people around. They laughed and carried on as they determinedly tried to make the couple feel intimidated and uneasy.

Within seconds both boys had removed their shoes and had dived into the dark water.

Perhaps they were used to people laughing at them or imitating them but the actions of the three seemed to have little effect. The two boys continued to enjoy the morning air and the anticipation of landing a second fish.

Their actions certainly began to frustrate Tran. He was not used to being ignored and was very determined to make his presence felt. He jumped to his feet and began mockingly waving his hands and then his whole arms around in a wild fashion. Suddenly, one of his feet got caught under his canvas chair and as it began to topple over the edge, he reached out to grab it.

Josh began running up the pier calling for help at the top of his voice. It was just as he was nearing the two boys that they looked up. They had heard nothing of his cries but at once recognised desperation on his pale face. His look of panic told a very brief but despairing story. As he pointed in the direction of the end of the pier, both boys dropped their rods and ran to where Sarita was crying hysterically, leaning over the edge of the old wooden platform.

Within seconds both boys had removed their shoes and had dived into the dark water. Eventually they resurfaced, supporting between them a gasping, terrified youth whose limbs seemed incapable of any movement. He was quite a weight for the boys as they hauled him up onto the rocks close to Roberto and Guiseppi's gear. Early morning strollers along the beach had heard the screams and had gathered in numbers to watch the valiant rescue. With encouragement and support from all around, Tran began to regain some strength and to everyone's relief, tried to sit up.

He lost his balance and with a terrified yell, fell to the water below. At this particular point the water was probably about four metres deep. His two comrades began screaming because, tough though they all were, none of them could swim. This was a fact that only became apparent as they yelled to others for help. 'Toughness' on land was clearly different from 'toughness' in the water.

The Hatman stood up but wasn't going to venture too close because he had never really communicated with the group and wasn't sure of their sincerity. Perhaps this was just another one of their attempts to make a fool out of him. Roberto and Guiseppi scrambled up from their rocks but seemed reluctant to go too close.

The screams from Josh and Sarita became more frantic as they saw their friend's head disappear below the surface of the water. Still there was no reaction from the newcomers, whose eyes were fixed on one of their bending rods.

A couple of the onlookers carried him to their car and, at his insistence, drove him home instead of to the nearby doctor's surgery. The two young rescuers headed back to their rods, gathered up their gear and headed home.

The next morning everything was the same down at the pier except for one thing.

The two young boys, Marcos and Fernando, sat alongside Josh, Tran and Sarita, right at the end of the pier.

— ◆◆◆ —

SILENT HEROES

Worksheet 1

1. Why do you think the two boys were referred to as 'strangers'?

   _____
   _____
   _____
   _____
   _____

2. Make a list of words that you think would describe the personalities of Josh, Tran and Sarita before the catastrophe took place.

   _____
   _____
   _____
   _____
   _____

3. Why do you think the three children 'targeted' the other people on the pier?

   _____
   _____

4. What indications were there in the text that encouraged you to think the two boys were 'different'?

   _____
   _____

5. Draw a line to the appropriate responses.

   Tran's accident ...

   | was the result of jealousy. | was what he deserved. | could have been avoided. | taught the three friends a lesson. | terrified his friends. |

6. Why didn't the strangers on the pier react when Josh and Sarita were screaming?

   _____
   _____
   _____
   _____

7. How did the actions of the boys change the attitudes of Tran, Josh and Sarita?

   _____
   _____
   _____
   _____

TRANSITION ISSUES   Prim-Ed Publishing   www.prim-ed.com

Worksheet 2: SILENT HEROES

1. Why do you think some people taunt others who are 'different' or have disabilities?

   _____
   _____

2. Do you know anyone with a disability? [YES | NO]

   If you do what problems, if any, do they encounter in their day-to-day life? How do they overcome these difficulties?

Problems encountered	How they are overcome

3. Do you think all people who are 'deaf' or 'blind' see themselves as being different? [YES | NO]

   Give reasons for your answer.

   _____
   _____
   _____
   _____

4. The two boys in the story were very happy. Do you think the fact that they both had the same disability had any bearing on this?

   [YES | NO] Explain your answer

   _____
   _____
   _____
   _____

5. If someone with a 'disability' was to move into your class or neighbourhood you could be responsible for making them feel 'accepted'. Write four sentences that you could say to this person to make him/her feel that you wanted to be a friend.

   a. _____
   b. _____
   c. _____
   d. _____

Prim-Ed Publishing   www.prim-ed.com   TRANSITION ISSUES

SILENT HEROES — Worksheet 3

1. Imagine that your class has been studying the human body. As part of your unit of work you have researched a number of physical and mental disabilities that people in our society are either born with or develop. One of your assessment tasks is to give an oral presentation on 'accepting people with differences'. Write a brief outline of six key areas you will address during your presentation. In the smaller boxes, draw a symbol that might help you recall the information in each case so that you will be able to focus on the audience rather than rely too much on your notes.

TRANSITION ISSUES   Prim-Ed Publishing   www.prim-ed.com   55

His speech was a little slurred because the muscles in his face didn't always do what he wanted, but the word 'thank you' was very audible.

JUST ONE OF US

During the last two weeks of autumn term we had noticed a number of workers around our school, changing the structure of entrances and making alterations around the toilet blocks and in some of the corridor areas. Being caught up in the excitement of Christmas activities we didn't even wonder why this was happening and just accepted that the school was obviously in need of some repair work.

When our first day of spring term arrived we were eventually told why the work had been done at the end of the previous year. Actually, there had been more extensive work completed over the holiday break. The next day we were to have a new boy arrive in our class. His name was Andre and he would be in a wheelchair.

Miss Lockwood, our teacher, spent a long time talking to us about Andre. She told us how during his birth he had been deprived of sufficient oxygen. This had caused what is known as cerebral palsy. Cerebral palsy can affect different parts of the brain to varying degrees and therefore the symptoms differ from one sufferer to the next. Miss Lockwood told us that Andre lacked muscular coordination and his legs were virtually paralysed. She showed us photographs of Andre in his wheelchair and she explained to us how he moved around and techniques he used in order to do his schoolwork.

As far as learning was concerned, Andre's brain worked just the same way as ours. For the first two years of his schooling he had attended a Special School but from the age of six he had attended Westfield Primary School in Birnleigh. Andre's dad had been transferred in his job and therefore the family had needed to move house. This was why he was to join our school community.

Miss Lockwood introduced us to a lady called Marianna. She was Andre's school assistant and would spend each day helping him inside and outside the classroom. She also spoke to us for quite a while explaining a bit more about Andre's appearance, about how it was a little difficult to understand some of the things he said, and she stressed how important it was that we didn't make him feel 'different'.

It was the subject of our conversations for the rest of the day. We had never before had anyone with such problems at our school. We questioned each other about where Andre might sit in the classroom, what he would do at break times and who might become his close friends.

Most of us saw Andre arrive the next morning. He came in a special taxi with his parents. Many children were watching. Apparently every classroom teacher had spoken to his or her class about Andre; not in the detail that we had been given, but every child in the school was aware of the fact that we were getting a new child who would be in a wheelchair. Everyone within view of the taxi was looking in that direction and it was obvious that most groups of children were discussing the new arrival.

The taxi driver lowered a special ramp from the rear of the car and immediately Andre was on the footpath he turned his chair in the direction of the school playground. We saw that he wasn't very big and he sat in the chair with his head tipped towards one shoulder. Marianna was at the gate to meet them and she immediately lifted up Andre's arm and shook his hand. She did the same to his parents and welcomed the three of them to Yarra Meadows School.

As we stood watching, Blake and Jackson walked up to Andre and also welcomed him. They explained that they were in his class, 6H, and that we were all looking forward to having him as part of our class group. Andre immediately thanked the boys. His speech was a little slurred because the muscles in his face didn't always do what he wanted, but the words 'thank you' were very audible.

It did take a little bit of time to get used to Andre being in our classroom. We had to make sure that the gaps between our tables were wide enough to fit the wheelchair. We also had to ensure that we never left things on the floor and it took us a while to get used to the way Andre spoke and the fact that Marianna was always with him.

Andre used a computer to do most of his work. He brought his own laptop with him and although he only had movement in some of his fingers, he amazed us because he was so good at using the keyboard. We learnt to listen extra carefully when Andre spoke and if ever he had too much difficulty getting a message across, he would explain things to Marianna who would then repeat them to us. This didn't happen very often though.

It didn't take us long to see how much Andre loved break time. This had been one of our major concerns – how could Andre ever play with us? Marianna spent most of the break outside with us but very soon she moved more and more to the sidelines, allowing us to assist Andre when and where he needed it. He actually had quite good movement in one arm and so he loved to have a turn at bowling in cricket. His bowls were quite gentle and not particularly accurate but none of us cared. He was great at cards and he was the best spectator you could ever want. He cheered us all on in sport, laughed at what we were doing and was always very eager to give us advice.

For the first week or so it was pretty noticeable that some children were very fascinated by Andre. There were always extra groups standing around watching us play. They particularly had their eyes on Andre. Most of them were only curious to see how he handled different situations. After a while, interest in us, and particularly our new friend, disappeared and they all went about their own activities in different areas of the playground.

Within a short time everyone in the school knew his name and there was hardly a person who passed him, including parents, who didn't stop or sing out some form of greeting.

Andre particularly loved music lessons. We were fortunate enough to have a music room at our school and every Thursday afternoon our class spent time with Mrs Browne, singing, dancing, listening to and creating music. Andre told us he would love to have played guitar but his coordination wouldn't allow for it but he was fantastic at keeping the beat with any percussion instrument. His singing wasn't too good, only because of his trouble with pronunciation, but that never stopped him from singing along with us.

During art lessons either Marianna or one of us would help him with anything he found particularly difficult such as using scissors or sharpening pencils. He found drawing a little difficult but he loved to paint.

Next year Andre and I will be going to the same secondary school. He really has become a special friend. I don't look at him and think about his differences, I just look at him and see him as 'one of us'.

JUST ONE OF US

Worksheet 1

1. What was wrong with Andre and how did this affect him?

   _____
   _____
   _____

2. Why do you think Miss Lockwood and Marianna spent so long speaking to the class about Andre?

   _____
   _____

3. What might children think if they were told they were going to have a classmate with the following disability?

	Disability	Children' thoughts/reactions
(a)	blindness	
(b)	deafness	
(c)	paralysis	

4. How do you think Blake and Jackson's reactions would have made Andre and his parents feel?

   _____
   _____

5. Fill in the boxes to outline different feelings experienced by the following people throughout the story.

Andre	Andre's parents	Other children	Marianna	Miss Lockwood

6. How did the other children help Andre cope with his move to a new school?

   _____
   _____

JUST ONE OF US

Worksheet 2

1. Do you think that it is important for children like Andre to be given the opportunity to be integrated into the general school system? [YES][NO] Explain.
   _____
   _____
   _____

2. What different reactions do you think children throughout the school might show if a child with a 'noticeable disability' were to become part of your school community?

3. If someone such as Andre were to become part of your class group, how do you think you, personally, could help him or her feel welcome and valued?
   _____
   _____
   _____
   _____
   _____
   _____
   _____
   _____
   _____

4. What do you think of the idea of a school assistant being present at all times in a classroom to help a child with specific difficulties or disabilities?
   _____
   _____
   _____

5. How is the term 'dumb' often misused in our society?
   _____
   _____
   _____

6. What other title might have been given to the story about Andre?
   _____
   _____

TRANSITION ISSUES Prim-Ed Publishing www.prim-ed.com

Worksheet 3: JUST ONE OF US

1. Using newspapers and magazines, cut out letters to create a message that reflects the title of the story about Andre; e.g. 'Everyone has the right to learn'. Glue your message in the space below.

2. Use your own ideas to complete this poem about 'acceptance'.

> Each of us has a title
> We've all been given a name
> In many ways we're different
> In others we're just the same.
>
> It doesn't matter at all
> _____
> _____
> _____
>
> So if someone enters your life
> _____
> _____
> _____

Teachers notes

Transition

Aim:

To help children:

- feel as comfortable and confident as possible about the move to secondary school,
- highlight issues that may be of a concern as they contemplate the transition to secondary school,
- work together to ensure the last stages of primary school are very enjoyable.

Contents

Teachers notes 61–62

Thoughts on transition 63–64

Worksheets 1–3 65–67

The weekly class meeting 68–69

Worksheets 1–3 70–72

TRANSITION ISSUES   Prim-Ed Publishing   www.prim-ed.com

Transition

Teachers notes

Discussion suggestions:

- Talk about the different schools children will be moving on to.
- Allow children with brothers, sisters or friends at secondary school to share some experiences.
- As a class, list the major changes that children will probably encounter in the coming year.
- Use Worksheets 1, 2 and 3 to promote discussion about moving from primary to secondary school.

Follow-up:

- Arrange for transition coordinators and former children to visit your class.
- Allocate time for class meetings or discussions related to the topic.
- Perhaps in the final weeks of the children's year the timetable could be changed to reflect a timetable similar to one that they will have the following year.

> • Remember, some children will be very confident about moving onto 'new ground' whereas others will be quite apprehensive.

Answers

Worksheet 1 – page 65

1. Teacher check

2. Answers may include:
   Meeting new children, more children, greater distance to travel, leaving home earlier, more homework, more teachers, working in different classrooms, collecting books for each lesson, needing to be more organised and responsible.

3–7. Teacher check

Worksheet 1 – page 70

1–6. Teacher check

THOUGHTS ON TRANSITION

PHILLIPPA had really been looking forward to being in her final year of primary school. For so long she had dreamt about playing interschool sport on Friday afternoons, about going to Camp Wilson and about having a leaving party.

As the summer term began to fly by, she couldn't believe that the year she had been so desperate to begin was rapidly drawing to a close. There was constant mention of moving onto secondary school, orientation days at secondary schools and graduation. Although Phillippa felt a certain excitement about all these events, they also caused her to feel a little uneasy.

Phillippa would be going to Warrenburn Secondary School next year. She had been to the school several times because her two older sisters were already there. She didn't verbalise her uneasiness to anyone but there were many different issues running through her mind.

Phillippa had been at the Rossmore Primary School for seven years. There were about 230 children at this school; at the secondary school there would be approximately 1100 children. Like most primary schools, all subjects at Rossmore, with the exception of music, were held in the one classroom. One teacher taught the majority of subjects to any class group and the primary school was only five minutes drive from Phillippa's home. Because of this closeness, Phillippa didn't have to leave for school until 8.45 a.m.

Warrenburn School was about 15 kilometres away so Phillippa would have to travel by train next year, needing to leave home at 7.40 a.m. What a change this would be to her relatively carefree mornings!

Homework had never caused her a problem. Most nights she only had one activity to do. If ever her teacher gave the class a major project, research and written presentation would take the place of other homework at least twice a week. Phillippa took great pride in her work but she wasn't particularly 'speedy'. Her teacher had begun telling the class that in secondary school, on any one night, they might have homework from three or four teachers and they could have several project requirements at the same time. Phillippa was finding it a bit difficult to imagine how she would cope with this increased workload.

Another matter that was playing on her mind, not really stressing her, but affecting her concentration at times, was the fact that she would be in a year level with approximately 160 other children. For seven years there had only been 30 children in her level and she knew them all so personally. Most of the children at Phillippa's primary school lived on her estate. At the secondary school, the children would come from many different areas, having undergone

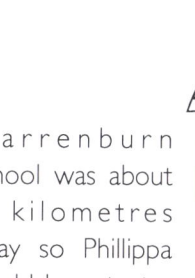

> There was constant mention of moving onto secondary school, orientation days at secondary schools and graduation.

many different life experiences. Although about 15 children would travel to the school with her, she wondered if she would make any new friends. If she did, what would they be like? Would they have the same interests? Would their families be just like her family?

As she looked around the classroom that had been her 'home' for almost a year, Phillippa pondered the idea of moving from room to room every 50 minutes or so. There would also be the added task of ensuring she'd taken the correct books from her locker prior to the commencement of each lesson.

This was the thing that her sister, Victoria, had found most challenging when she'd begun secondary school, but, Victoria admitted herself, she lacked organisational skills. At least Phillippa was very organised.

In two weeks the transition coordinator from Warrenburn would be coming to talk to all the children who would be moving to that school next year. After a talk by the coordinator there would be time for questions. As well as the coordinator, several children who had previously attended Rossmore Primary would be there to share their experiences. Phillippa was hoping that by the time the session was over she and the other children going to Warrenburn would have discussed and found answers to many of the questions that were floating around in their minds. Their own teacher had already assured them that most children, when about to move from primary school to secondary school, felt the same. One thing Phillippa kept telling herself was that if her disorganised sister could survive this transition there was little doubt that she too would be able to cope!

THOUGHTS ON TRANSITION

Worksheet 1

1. Why do you think most children see their final year of primary school as such a special year?
   _____
   _____
   _____
   _____
   _____
   _____

2. What major differences are often faced when moving from primary to secondary school?
   _____
   _____
   _____
   _____
   _____
   _____

3. Make a list of words that would describe Phillippa's feelings as she pondered life at secondary school.

4. Do you think having an older relative at the secondary school a child is moving onto would be an advantage?
   [YES | NO] Explain.
   _____
   _____
   _____
   _____

5. Why do you think transition coordinators from secondary schools often visit primary schools during that final year?
   _____
   _____
   _____
   _____
   _____
   _____

6. Do you think it would be important for Phillippa to ask questions when the transition coordinator came to visit?
   [YES | NO] Explain.
   _____
   _____
   _____

7. Do you think Phillippa's feelings would be unique to her?
   [YES | NO] Explain.
   _____
   _____
   _____
   _____

TRANSITION ISSUES   Prim-Ed Publishing   www.prim-ed.com

THOUGHTS ON TRANSITION

1. Why do some people experience feelings of both excitement and trepidation as the move to secondary school approaches?

   _____

   _____

   _____

2. What experiences are you most looking forward to at secondary school?

3. What things are you a little nervous about now that secondary school life is not far away?

4. When the transition coordinator from your secondary school comes to visit, what questions do you think you would like to ask?

   _____

   _____

   _____

   _____

5. How important do you think it is to enjoy the end of your final year at primary school?

   |⊢_____|_____⊣|
   not important   **very important**

   Give reasons for your answer.

   _____

   _____

   _____

6. Who do you think you will speak to next year if you encounter any problems while settling in to secondary school?

   _____

THOUGHTS ON TRANSITION

1. Think about the six most fantastic memories you have of your time at primary school. Number them in order from most to least significant experience.

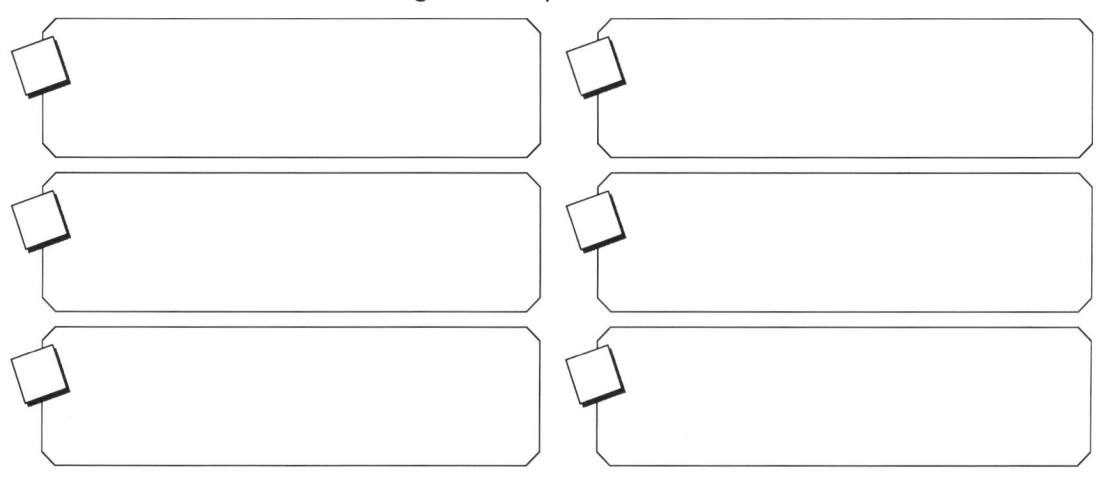

   ☐ _____   ☐ _____

   ☐ _____   ☐ _____

   ☐ _____   ☐ _____

2. Think of six things that you are most looking forward to experiencing at secondary school. Number them in order from the experiences you are most looking forward to.

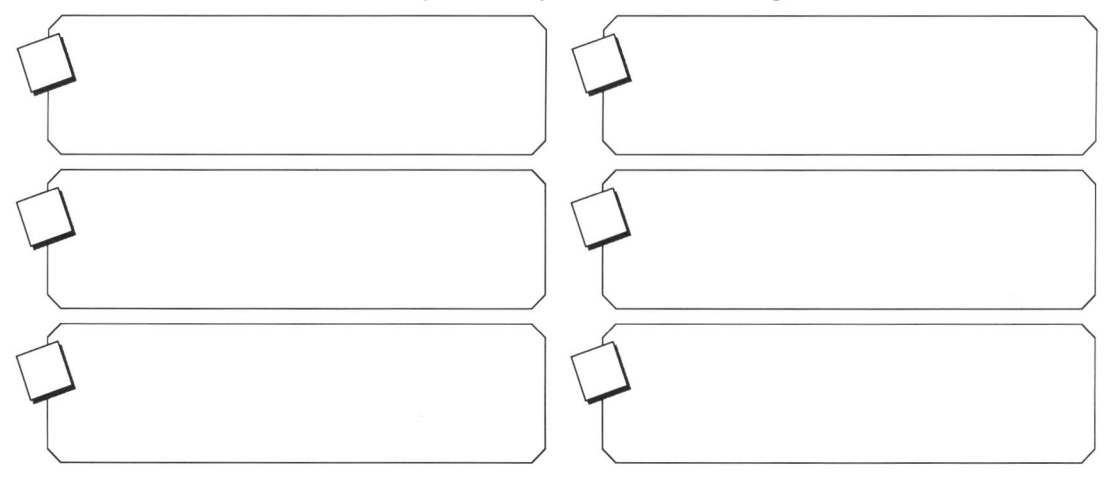

   ☐ _____   ☐ _____

   ☐ _____   ☐ _____

   ☐ _____   ☐ _____

3. In the space below, write an inspirational statement about the move from primary to secondary school; e.g. 'Moving on towards new horizons'.

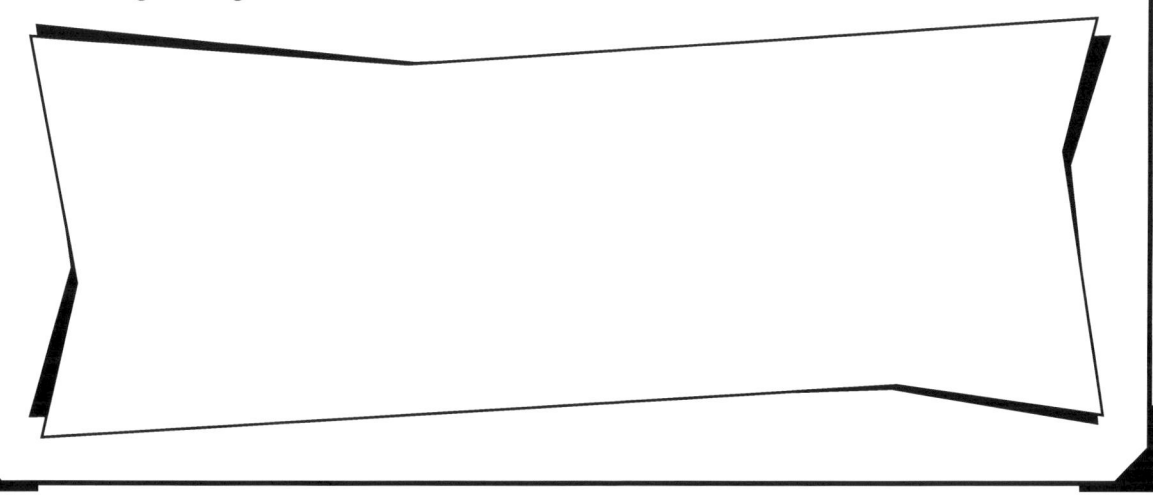

The Weekly Class Meeting

ON THE FIRST DAY of our final term in primary school, Mr Yahn began what was to become a weekly event. Every Monday between break and lunchtime we have a class meeting. It's a pretty formal meeting, chaired by our class captains and there are special routines in place if any of us want a particular topic discussed during a meeting. Each Tuesday, a sheet is placed on one of our notice boards. It has a heading, 'Topics to be discussed at forthcoming meeting'. We have until the following Friday to write down any issues that we wish raised at the next class meeting.

Last week, apart from a brief discussion about our roster for emptying the rubbish bins, the whole meeting was centred around moving on to secondary school. Many people in the class raised issues they had heard about from older brothers and sisters or friends or that we had actually been tossing around among ourselves. Sam said that his brother had found it a bit challenging going from the 'top' of the primary school to the 'bottom' of the secondary school.

As Darcie pointed out, we are constantly being called school leaders. We have taken on roles such as school and sport captains, child representative council members and peer support leaders. Next year we won't be holding any of these positions and it could be a little bit of a let-down.

Olivia said that at the school where her brother goes, all first year children belong to a peer support group that is led by an older child. She said that this is a fantastic idea because the older children are carefully chosen for the role and they really work at helping the first years feel important. Mr Yahn was quick to jump in and tell us to enjoy this type of experience. As he said, this has been a full-on year with little time for rest and there have constantly been additional expectations and responsibilities placed upon us.

Stefan has three brothers at the local secondary school and he told us that there are plenty of things we could become involved in without having to take on a leadership role. There are many extracurricular activities such as choirs, bands, sports teams and debating teams that we can join. Once again Mr Yahn had a reassuring point to make. He said that through being involved in such activities we could very easily develop leadership skills that could aid us in future years.

When Andre brought up the subject of friendship you could see that we all thought this was an important issue. Some of us will be moving on to schools with a number of our peers but there are some who will be going by themselves to more distant schools. Andre pointed out that as a class we've all got along pretty well for seven years and it seems strange that by this time next year we might have developed completely different circles of friends. Mr Yahn said that he often met with coordinators from the secondary schools and he said they had told him that they all tend to have a first year camp within the first few weeks of the school year. Many of the activities undertaken on these camps require cooperative learning, where those involved need to develop trust in each other and also offer continual assistance to team members. During these activities many new friendship bonds begin to develop.

By the time the bell went for lunch last Monday we were all feeling that the step from primary to secondary school would not be too daunting. We decided that two more meetings during the term would be set aside for the specific aim of addressing the importance of this transition stage. Just before our class captains officially closed the meeting, Mr Yahn said something that really stuck in my mind. He told us that secondary school opens up a whole new world of experiences, challenges and opportunities.

When I was telling Mum about our meeting that night she said she agreed wholeheartedly with what Mr Yahn had said. She said that just because we were putting on new uniforms and going to new environments, didn't mean that our enjoyment of learning would change or our desire to be with friends. I think I'm really starting to get excited about the prospect of moving to Cambridge Heights Secondary School.

TRANSITION ISSUES **Prim-Ed Publishing** www.prim-ed.com

THE WEEKLY CLASS MEETING

1. List four reasons why such class meetings could prove very beneficial.

2. Why might some children find it difficult moving from the 'top' of the primary school to the 'bottom' of the secondary school?

3. What would you regard as the four most significant advantages of having the school camp early in the year?

4. Do children have to change the way they approach their learning just because they move to secondary school? **YES** **NO** Explain.

5. If your class was to hold one of these meetings, what would you like to have discussed?

6. Do you think peer support groups sound like a good idea? **YES** **NO** Explain.

THE WEEKLY CLASS MEETING

1. As this year draws to a close, do you think it would be beneficial for your class to hold a couple of meetings at which you could all discuss your expectations, excitement and concerns regarding the move into secondary school? [YES] [NO] Explain.

   _____
   _____
   _____

2. Do you think people expect 'more' of your class because you are at the 'top' of the school? [YES] [NO] If so, in what way?

   _____
   _____
   _____

3. List three ways in which you think a secondary school could make its new children feel very welcome.

4. (a) How do you feel about meeting many new 'friends' next year?

   (b) Do you think you will maintain most of your current school friendships?

5. Do you think you would be happy to share your positive and negative feelings about secondary school at a class meeting? [YES] [NO] Explain.

   _____
   _____

TRANSITION ISSUES Prim-Ed Publishing www.prim-ed.com

THE WEEKLY CLASS MEETING

Worksheet 3

1. You are to chair the next class meeting that has been allocated to discuss transition to secondary school. When you look at all the suggestions children have made for the discussion you realise you could never fit them all into one meeting. Draw up an agenda below that you believe will cover the most important issues.

2. You are to conduct an interview with a transition coordinator. In each of the boxes is a topic about which you have to formulate a question. Write the questions you will ask.

Homework	**Number of lessons a day**
Lockers	**Sports uniform**

Prim-Ed Publishing   www.prim-ed.com   **TRANSITION ISSUES**

Teachers notes

Marriage breakdown

Aim:

To help children:

- understand that some marriages do break down,
- understand that children do not 'cause' their parents to separate or divorce,
- develop strategies to cope when going through the stress of their parents' separation.

Contents

Teachers notes 73–74

Far away on Father's Day 75–76

Worksheets 1–3 77–79

It's all my fault 80–81

Worksheets 1–3 82–84

Marriage breakdown

Teachers notes

Discussion suggestions:

- Ask children what they believe constitutes a family. (Direct the discussion towards the fact that not all family members live together all of the time.)
- Discuss the feelings of children at times when they know the relationship between their parents is not good.
- Keep trying to reinforce that the separation of parents doesn't mean that one parent no longer loves the child/children.
- Use Worksheets 1, 2 and 3 to promote discussion about marriage breakdown.

Follow-up:

- Closely monitor the effects that a marriage breakdown is having on a child.
- If necessary, arrange meetings with parents and children.

• Remember that some children will be ready to blame themselves for the problems being faced by others. Have your 'door open' when it's needed.

Answers

Worksheet 1 – page 77

1. Teacher check
2. Dad didn't attend the end of year pre-school concert, Mum crying, Dad taking his clothes.
3. Teacher check
4. He would like Dad to choose a present to send him.
5. Tory lives with him grandpa.
6. Teacher check
7. Teacher check

Worksheet 1 – page 82

1. Teacher check
2. Teacher check
3. Teacher check
4. Answers may include:
   They stopped going out for dinner on Fridays, became more serious with and ignored each other. They raised their voices and argued about money.
5. Dad said he couldn't afford her school fees.
6. Teacher check
7. They thought they had betrayed and failed her, causing her pain.
8. She believes that they love her and never wanted to hurt her.

FAR AWAY ON FATHER'S DAY

Everyone was really excited when we came into the classroom this morning, except for me. Inside everyone's school bag was a plastic supermarket bag. These bags were to hide the presents that would be purchased at the Father's Day stall. What was the point of me bringing a bag? My dad lives somewhere abroad and I haven't seen him for more than two years. I wouldn't even know where to send the present if I bought one.

My mum and dad split up when I was four years old. I can't remember much about when it happened but I can remember being really sad when Dad couldn't come to the end-of-year concert at pre-school. Mum was crying that night but she said it was because I was such a funny Rudolph the Red-nosed Reindeer that she was crying tears of laughter. I don't think she was telling the truth. I know it was just the weekend after that my dad took all his clothes away in a suitcase.

> Maybe one day I'll see my dad again. I guess he still loves me. Mum often tells me he does but sometimes it's hard to imagine.

When I was seven I went for a holiday to Dad's house. It was about four hours drive away from where we lived. That's when I met Jenny. My Dad told me that he was going to marry Jenny and that they were going to live a long way away in a different country. Jenny was okay but I think she really tried to be too nice. My mum is just naturally nice. That was the last time I saw my dad.

When he first moved abroad he used to phone me every now and then but he doesn't do that any more. He still sends me birthday and Christmas cards and he always puts a cheque inside them. I wish he would send me a present that he had chosen by himself.

I have a photo of my dad on my bedside table and I know my nose looks just like his. It's a pretty old photo because it was taken on my 6th birthday. He's wearing my party hat which has a huge red 6 on the front. I sometimes wonder what my mum thinks about when she picks up the photo frame and dusts it.

Tory doesn't have a dad. His dad died of cancer last year when we were nine. I guess the two of us can go to the Fathers' Day stall together and do what Mrs Quilty suggested. She's our class teacher and she said that we could buy a present for our grandpas. Tory lives with his grandpa so that's probably why he was pretty excited about the stall. Both my grandfathers live a long way from our house so I won't even see them on Sunday.

I think I might actually buy a present for Uncle Garry. He's Mum's brother and he and his wife are really good to us. They only live about 20 minutes drive from our house and Uncle Garry is always ready to help Mum with difficult tasks. I think he would really appreciate a present from me. We are going to their place for lunch on Sunday.

Sometimes Uncle Garry seems to sense that I miss having a dad around. He has three daughters and I really think he'd like a son because he takes me to football matches and is always eager to come to my school if we're having a special night for our dads.

This afternoon when we make Father's Day cards I think I'll make one for Uncle Garry. It's not quite the same as being able to make one for my dad like the other kids will be doing, but it's still for a very special person. I already know what I'll put inside. I'll write an acrostic poem.

Maybe one day I'll see my dad again. I guess he still loves me. Mum often tells me that he does but sometimes it's hard to imagine. If he really loved me wouldn't he want to see me, especially on Father's Day?

U understanding
N never stops caring
C can play football
L loves our family
E enjoys my company

G greatest uncle in the world
A Auntie Julie loves him
R really, really funny
R really, really bad at singing
Y you are my best friend

FAR AWAY ON FATHER'S DAY

Worksheet 1

1. Do you think there was anything that could have been done to prevent the author feeling as he did when he walked into the classroom that morning?

   [YES] [NO] List some suggestions.

   _____
   _____
   _____

2. What distant memories did he have of when his parents split up?

   _____
   _____
   _____

3. According to your own feelings, rank the following.

   (a) The importance of parents maintaining contact with their children even when separated.

   |⊢—————————————————⊢—————————————————⊣|
   not important   **extremely important**

   (b) The importance of teachers being made aware of family situations such as separation.

   |⊢—————————————————⊢—————————————————⊣|
   not important   **extremely important**

4. Why does the author seem a little disappointed with the cheques that are included in the birthday and Christmas cards?

   _____
   _____

5. Why was it likely that Tory would want to buy a present for his grandpa?

   _____
   _____
   _____

6. How important do you think Uncle Garry is in the young author's life?

   _____
   _____
   _____

7. Did you think it was a good idea for him to buy a present for Uncle Garry at the Father's Day stall? [YES] [NO] Explain.

   _____
   _____
   _____

FAR AWAY ON FATHER'S DAY

Worksheet 2

1. Make a list of words that might describe how a child would feel when first told that his/her parents were going to split up.

2. What times of the year are probably most difficult for children who do not have both parents living at home?

3. If parents split up, what special message do you think they should both be giving to their children?

   _____
   _____
   _____

4. If one parent lives a long way away, how can a child maintain a special form of communication with that parent?

   _____
   _____

5. Do you think children actually get used to the fact that their parents live apart?
   [YES][NO] Explain.

   _____
   _____
   _____

6. Apart from their parents, who else might children choose to talk to when they are upset about a marriage break-up?

   _____
   _____
   _____
   _____

7. How do you think classroom teachers can be sensitive to the feelings of children in these situations?

   _____
   _____
   _____
   _____

Prim-Ed Publishing   www.prim-ed.com   TRANSITION ISSUES

FAR AWAY ON FATHER'S DAY

Worksheet 3

Decorate this card and inside write a special message to your dad or mum, expressing how you feel about him/her.

For My

'I've caused my mum and dad to split up!'

IT'S ALL MY FAULT

MY NAME IS BRINDA and I am 13 years old. Last week I felt like my insides were being torn apart. I was unable to concentrate on anything other than the massive problem that I believed I had caused. As I tried desperately to resolve the issue eating away at my mind I pulled away from everyone and everything. Feeling emotionally at 'rock-bottom' I sought help from someone who, in the past, I had thought I would never have to visit. Miss Veldo is our school psychologist. Her office is located close to the main school administration office and is next to the headteacher's and deputy headteacher's offices. Being only new to the school, I had very few reasons to venture into this part of the school. I was trembling as I knocked on Miss Veldo's door at lunchtime last Wednesday. When she asked me to go in I literally felt sick in my stomach. Seeing a huge amount of paperwork on her desk, I asked if I could come back to see her at some time the following day.

I don't know whether it was the look on my face or the fact that my whole body seemed to be trembling, but Miss Veldo told me that she was more than happy to chat to me right there and then. Pushing her work to one side she told me to take a seat. I perched myself right on the edge of the seat as though I was preparing to make a quick escape. Before she even got to ask me what I wanted to see her about I blurted out,

'I've caused my mum and dad to split up!'

The look on Miss Veldo's face reflected both amazement and concern. As she carried her chair around to my side of the table to sit beside me, tears began streaming down my face. Because of the mixture of remorse, fear and anxiety that had been building up inside me, I was like a dormant volcano that had come back to life. Putting her hand on my shoulder, Miss Veldo tried to convince me that it couldn't possibly be my fault. She asked me how I knew that my parents were splitting up. Like a rush of lava I found I couldn't stop talking once I found some deep-seated courage.

I began by telling her that Mum and Dad used to go out to dinner every Friday night. About three months ago they stopped doing this and they gave me a variety of excuses as to why they no longer went to restaurants or the theatre: one of them wasn't feeling well, Dad had to go to work early on Saturday morning, the car was in getting a service, whatever. For a while these excuses seemed legitimate enough, but then I began noticing how they were all pretty trivial. I'd also noticed that my parents were becoming more and more serious with each other, often not even acknowledging that the other one was sitting at the same meal table.

Occasionally, I'd asked each of them independently what was wrong, but I was always given a cheery response that made me feel that I was worrying about nothing at all. A few times at night I'd heard them raise their voices at each other but I never really knew what the conversations were about. I did hear the bank get mentioned a couple of times.

Still shaking, I went on to tell Miss Veldo how, the night before, I had heard a lot more of one of their loud discussions. I'd heard my father say to my mother that it was all her idea to send me to this school. He'd said that it was nothing but money, money, money and that he'd had enough. He could no longer afford to pay for my schooling and he no longer wanted to live with us.

I told her how I'd cried all night because of how I'd made my dad feel. I believed that it was my fault that he had run out of money and that he didn't want to be a part of our family any more. Even though both Mum and Dad had tried to reassure me in the morning, I knew that things were never again going to be the same in my family. As I stopped to catch my breath, I began tracing back over the past three months, putting things into a new perspective. I remembered how I'd had to pay for my school camp a little later than most children and I thought about how Dad had encouraged me to buy a much cheaper brand of trainers than I'd ever had.

Miss Veldo and I talked for an hour and a half, ignoring bells to return to class and arranging a time when we could meet together with my parents. Miss Veldo said that it was most important that my parents were made aware of how I was feeling. She said that parents were usually devastated when they heard that their children were carrying such feelings inside themselves.

On Monday, the four of us met in Miss Veldo's office and, as I had been warned, my parents were shattered when I told them how I was feeling. They felt they had betrayed me and failed me terribly. They kept reassuring me of their unconditional love and said that the problems they were facing were because of things they alone had said and done.

I left the meeting feeling very relieved but still greatly saddened by the obvious dwindling of good feeling between my mum and dad. Dad told me he was going to move into a flat but not too far away. Because of their financial problems, Miss Veldo was going to meet with the school administration team to explain the situation and to ensure that I could remain at the school. She told my parents that this was particularly important because school was a very secure place for me. At school I was surrounded by friends and people who were supportive and encouraging.

Perhaps my parents will never get back together, but now I definitely believe that they both love me and that they never want to cause me such hurt again. I'm going to continue to visit Miss Veldo each week, just until I feel comfortable within myself.

◆◆◆

Worksheet 1: IT'S ALL MY FAULT

1. Why do you think many schools employ school psychologists?

   _____
   _____
   _____

2. What thoughts do you think would have flashed through the psychologist's mind when Brinda first told her what she 'had done'?

   _____
   _____
   _____

3. Fill in the remaining boxes with 'titles' of people a child might choose to speak to if a large crisis takes place in his/her life.

psychologist				
		form/class teacher		

4. What things had Brinda noticed about her parents' relationship?

   _____
   _____
   _____
   _____

5. What made her believe she was responsible for her parents' separation?

   _____
   _____
   _____
   _____

6. Do you think it was important that the psychologist ignored the bells and kept Brinda talking? [YES | NO] Explain.

   _____
   _____
   _____
   _____

7. Why were her parents devastated when told how Brinda was feeling?

   _____
   _____

8. What does Brinda believe her parents' feelings are towards her?

   _____
   _____

IT'S ALL MY FAULT

1. Do you believe children are ever responsible for a marriage break-up? [YES] [NO] Explain.
   _____
   _____
   _____

2. Why might children believe that they did play a part in their parents' separation?
   _____
   _____
   _____

3. If children do have these feelings, to whom could they speak?
   _____
   _____
   _____

4. (a) Do you think parents should be 'open' with their children and inform them when they are having problems?
   [YES] [NO]

   (b) Do you think the age of the children would have a bearing on this?
   [YES] [NO] Explain.
   _____
   _____
   _____
   _____

5. Despite their own problems, what is the most important thing that parents should have their children believe?
   _____
   _____
   _____
   _____
   _____
   _____
   _____

6. Do you think it is important for a teacher to be made aware of the fact that a child's family is going through some time of major crisis? [YES] [NO] Explain.
   _____
   _____
   _____
   _____

Worksheet 3 — IT'S ALL MY FAULT

1. All families are different. Rule the space below into a number of sections according to how many members are in your family. At the top of each space, write the name of one family member. Fill the space with all the wonderful things that person means to you.

2. Complete the following to create very positive statements about aspects of family life.

Parents should always ...

Each family member can be responsible for ...

Respect and understanding ...

Being a good listener ...

Prim-Ed Publishing   www.prim-ed.com   **TRANSITION ISSUES**